Liberation Is Imperative

How to Escape Corporate Slavery and
Create a Life of Freedom

Kevin Knight

10-10-10 Publishing
Markham, ON
Canada

Copyright © 2016 by Kevin Knight
First Edition

For further reading, please visit:
www.liberationisimperative.com

All rights reserved. No part of this publication may be reproduced, stored in a retrieval system, or transmitted, in any form or by any means, electronic, mechanical, photocopying, recording, or otherwise without the prior written permission from the publisher.

For information about special discounts for bulk purchases, please contact Liberation Is Imperative Special Sales at 800-515-5244 or business@liberationisimperative.com.

While the author has made best efforts to determine the source of all quotes contained herein, when a quote is commonly attributed to two people, the author has not included a definitive source.

This publication is designed to provide accurate and authoritative information in regard to the subject matter covered. It is sold with the understanding that the publisher is not engaged in rendering legal, accounting, or other professional services. If you require legal advice or other expert assistance, you should seek the services of a competent professional.

ISBN: 978-1-77277-071-1
ISBN: 978-1-77277-086-5 (ebook)

Contents

Acknowledgments	vii
Foreword	ix
Introduction	xi
Chapter 1 - Captivity in Complacency	1
Chapter 2 - Mental Warfare: The Battle Within	19
Chapter 3 - Relentless Positive Action: Never Quit!	37
Chapter 4 - Blessed & Highly Favored: Know Your Worth	55
Chapter 5 - Emancipation of the Subconscious	69
Chapter 6 - Faith, Vision & Purpose	83
Chapter 7 - Family Refuge	99
Chapter 8 - Absolute Urgency	113
Chapter 9 - Stand on Integrity	127
Chapter 10 - Leave a Legacy	141
About the Author	153

DEDICATION

This book is dedicated to the memory of my late sister, Carol. Love always.

ACKNOWLEDGMENTS

I was extremely blessed to have the support and guidance of many wonderful people to whom I want to express my sincere gratitude:

To my beautiful wife, Yunuen, who shared my vision and passion for this book and supported me whole heartedly. Te amo.

To my wonderful children, Sophia, Camila, Ayden, Tyler and Olivia. Daddy loves you.

To my family, Mommy, Daddy, Marcia, Nicole and Lawrence. Thank you for all your love, encouragement, and prayers. I love you.

To Raymond Aaron, for his words of wisdom.

To Cara Witvoet, my book architect, for her helpful insight and positive attitude throughout this entire project.

Kevin Knight

To Tracy Knepple, my editor, for her feedback and expertise.

Special thanks to my friend, Tavis Smiley, for his support.

And finally, to the many individuals who have in their own special ways supported me throughout the creation of this book: Rachael Boyer, Neal Tyler, Linda Salas, Terry Claybon, Joseph Pham, Laura Duong, Yvette Price, Brandon Manumaleuna, Will Bellamy, Grace Oh, Kiyoko Ando, Krishaun Gilmore, Adriel Roman, Kasey Kaehlert, Kenqin Zhong and Dayna Granger.

FOREWORD

I feel honored and privileged to have this opportunity to introduce you to Kevin Knight's book. His dedication to challenging the injustices and changing the culture within this world by starting with inner change to invoke a movement is both remarkable and commendable. *Liberation Is Imperative* is a vital tool. It is not only a practical primer, but a way of understanding the elements to finding your vision.

Far too often you play victim to the circumstances you encounter throughout your life. This is where the amazing book, *Liberation Is Imperative* will come into effect in your life. It lays out the major foundations that should be established for you looking to create your own destiny. Kevin outlines triumphant tactics for self-efficacy; a process that you, the reader, will soon experience for yourself as you read through the pages ahead.

Among the many profound revelations, Kevin reveals to you a fundamental approach to harnessing faith and believing in your dreams. Reading this inspiring book will help you break out of your mediocrity and negative-mindset and get you onto a new exhilarating passionate path of divine purpose and a life of freedom. I suggest you read it well and take a step toward truly living a life you love.

Raymond Aaron
New York Times Bestselling Author

INTRODUCTION

*"Leaving comfort and security then stepping out
into the unknown - that is liberation."*

We all have our comfort zone. The place where you feel that life cannot infringe upon your flow. A structured lifestyle where you can almost predict what will happen from one day to the next. A source of stability that provides a deep sense of security, and there is nothing wrong with that. There is nothing wrong with being satisfied with your job or being comfortable with your personal possessions or achievements.

It becomes a problem when you become complacent about your divine purpose within this world and your comfortable living invades your mental where about. Causing you to have a delusional and unknowing mindset to what you are destined to be. You should never reach a place in life where you are totally satisfied with the progress within yourself.

"There is an eagle in me that wants to soar, and there is a hippopotamus in me that wants to wallow in the mud."
- Carl Sandburg

We live in a world where there is no true certainty, as anything we hold dear can be taken away from us.

For most people, you are living a life based on the influence of others who may or may not have your best interests at hand. So you went out and created a life based on mental conditioning that made you believe that was what you were supposed to become.

In this book, I discuss how you can rise above the mediocrity within your life and start living in alignment with your core values and character. By focusing on the primary elements and requirements to overcome obstacles and engaging your own creativity, you can develop an expansive mindset that propels you to greatness.

If you feel you are not growing like you should, or are not satisfied with where you are right now, it doesn't have to be that way. Challenge yourself to make the necessary changes in your life today.

So let's embark on the journey necessary to excavate your vision, helping you to realize your true passion and run after your dreams. Caution! It doesn't always put you in a comfortable position. And that's okay.

CHAPTER 1

CAPTIVITY IN COMPLACENCY

"Complacency is the deadly enemy of spiritual progress. The contented soul is the stagnant soul."
- Aiden Wilson Tozer

BLINDSIDED BY LIFE

In a moment, life as you know it can be altered. One is reminded of that when a loved one has suddenly passed on, a job is taken without notice or reason, or a fatal diagnosis is given. At the time of the event, it can be peculiar and disconcerting. In some form, it is life's way of asking, "What are you made of?" How will this event define you? Will you retreat into your emotional bomb shelter and yield to the circumstances, allowing them to dictate your existence? Or will you engage it head on and transform into a powerful being that can harness those circumstances for the benefit of others?

Yes, it's easy to become indignant when faced with the mysteries of life and the unjustifiable suffering that takes place in this world. One of the biggest challenges in life is to avoid discounting your self-worth or value. You don't know who you are until you are really tested. So live life expecting the unexpected with the preconceived notion that every event you encounter is meant to empower you. Because it's your thoughts that become your feelings, and your feelings become your energy, which shifts to your conscious awareness and your actions. When trials and tribulations come, they will reveal what is truly inside your heart.

Make it a practice today to start resisting the crutch of comfort. It takes security in one's self-worth to acknowledge discouragement but not be defeated. This will allow you to acquire a renewed determination and resilience towards cataclysmic challenges. You then take on life obstacles as challenges to be overcome and define them as opportunities.

It is also important for you to understand that one should never be too comfortable and overconfident, naively trusting of others, or fail to properly evaluate the environment around you. Life is dynamic, so you must be willing and able to adjust or you will be psychologically extinct. I will cover this in detail later on in this chapter.

There is no logical answer to the mysteries of unforeseen pain or tribulations in life. But what we do know is that they will produce a passion and purpose within, if you are open to allowing it to manifest. Do not make the mistake that so many do of focusing more on the outer circumstances rather than the internal conditioning. Start by scrupulously identifying your low-level thoughts, feelings and disbeliefs, which hinder you from your greatness.

You must wake up every morning knowing that no matter what unknown influential circumstances may unveil themselves, you are totally responsible for the meaning and power given to them. When I am a guest speaker on-stage, the event host loves when I break down the steps to counter attacking being blindsided to the audience. It's all a matter of constructing a solid foundation and action plan, then living into them intentionally. This will shape your perspective to face any adversity.

Be warned. The journey you are about to take part in may be thought provoking to you, but it's never too late to improve and make changes within your life. All you have to do is make the decision to simply live with defined intentions.

ALLOWING APATHY TO RULE

When one becomes indifferent to the needs of themselves and the society they were created to serve, the door is opened to living a life of mediocrity. Passion is relinquished and you're a walking living death sentence. You're completely satisfied with working in a mundane job serving a 15 to 25-year sentence with the possibility of pension and retirement. You've surrounded yourself with energy draining relationships that are not empowering you. You're neglecting enhancing your mind state and physical well-being. This is truly a calamity, because no one was designed to be mediocre.

The key is not to wait for the motivation to come and apathy to dissipate. In order to escape the mundane, you need to engage in your freedom of expression. Allow yourself to be inquisitive, imaginative and uninhibited to the wonders of life. This will bring you to a place of exploration deep down inside. The state of wonder is where you will find your heart's true desire.

Understand that you don't have to be an overnight success and accomplish all your goals at once. Allow momentum to build naturally by taking it one action step at a time. Commit to one single positive change that will impact your psyche, and then do it every day until it becomes a habit. Once you've mastered that new habit, add another, then rinse and repeat this cycle as part of your lifestyle.

Consistently focusing on one goal at a time will help you maintain the energy and motivation needed to accomplish it. This will also inspire you to know that when you have laser focus, carrying out any challenging task is possible. Don't only look at how far you have to go but how far you have come. It's about incremental improvement within your daily life and mental habits.

Once you learn what you want and have begun taking healthy action to achieve it, you need to maintain a willing and eager state of being. In order to do this, you need to invest time into appreciating your improvements. Do not take yourself and what you've done for granted. Review and relish in what you've created by simply applying your will to it. You then build a stronger bond to your passion and goals, as well as build trust in yourself that you can improve your life no matter what. Set your goals and make a plan to achieve them one by one. It will make you accountable for your own results. As you strive to achieve them, you can undoubtedly expect that there will be setbacks and disappointments. Don't be dismayed, the road to your dreams is never an easy one. This is where laser focus and diligence will aid you in battling the winds of change. Remember no matter where the path will lead you, it's the right direction. Let go of expectations of how the process should look. Realignment is a part of the journey.

If you have not been enlightened to the theme within these insights, it's you. Apathy needs your permission to have a kingly seat within your mindset. Stay alert to when comfort sets in and you're not raising the bar, but instead are settling in life. Bowing down to tough moments and not believing in yourself. Giving up today means you are creating a limited tomorrow. Not using your pain to fuel you to success. Not taking responsibility for the challenges that life throws in your way. How will you serve the world if you don't have the faith to know that you are deserving of a life of abundance?

No one besides yourself can convince you to rise from the monotony and push forward to your destiny. Do not lose sight of your dreams and their importance in your life and the world. The next step is to go out and take action with real desire, even when you don't feel like it. Make a decision not to give into the humdrum of everyday life. In order to have a victorious, powerful, positive life and escape a listless life, you must be willing to work hard for the triumph of your limitless possibilities.

CREATURE OF HABIT

The person you are and will become derive from your habits. They provide structure and discipline to your life. Your habits, good or bad, will reinforce themselves, when your will power deteriorates. It's in the private discipline of habits where battles are either won or loss. Habits come from repetition; what you did yesterday, you will do today whether it is necessarily a positive or negative decision.

I often share this story with my audiences to illustrate what the perils of squandering the opportunity to change can create. A wealthy man requested an old scholar to wean his son away from his bad habits. The scholar took the youth for a stroll through a garden. Stopping suddenly, he asked the boy to pull out a tiny plant growing there. The youth held the plant between his thumb and forefinger and pulled it out. The old man then asked him to pull out a slightly bigger plant. The youth pulled hard and the plant came out, roots and all. "Now pull out that one," said the old man pointing to a bush. The boy had to use all his strength to pull it out. "Now take this one out," said the old man, indicating a guava tree. The youth grasped the trunk and tried to pull it out. But it would not budge. "I – It's impossible," said the boy, panting with the effort. "So it is with bad habits," said the sage. "When they are young, it is easy to pull them out, but when they take hold they cannot be uprooted." The session with the old man changed the boy's life. I see the moral in this story being one of allowing non supportive habits to take root and control you. When attempting to overcome bad habits, it will require authentically working on developing character to break these destructive habits. It will also require changes in lifestyle. Old habits can and must be changed. New ones must be created at the deep subconscious level in order to have control over your destiny.

Your visceral fauna is to naturally do what is easy. Feeling contented in life and your accomplishments is the difference between what you should do versus what you actually do. Life controlling habits are formed at a pace that is almost unnoticeable. Unbeknownst to many, small choices you make every day may also disturb your mindset more than you may realize. When you nurture destructive habits, it has a direct correlation to wrong beliefs and attitudes. There will be limited success in developing supportive habits until you discover the greater purpose for your life. Truly admit what you are doing or thinking is wrong. Don't justify your present ways and refuse to see the damage you are causing to yourself or others. Recognize and control self-defeating thoughts.

Change is inconvenient because people are afraid of the unknown. Our society has conditioned you to believe that the unknown in life is like walking to the edge of the earth and then falling into tormenting and dangerous terrain. Walking into the unknown is what has helped us evolve as a civilization, taken us beyond the outer limits. Digging down deep within yourself and taking a leap of faith, then walking and living by it, will help you break the stronghold of any destructive habit at any point in your life. The question you need to ask yourself is, do you want to enter into your greatness now or just exist as a slave working for a living?

When you take this risk and accept that damaging habits must submit to your prevailing affirmative actions, a feeling of freedom enters into your life. Habits can no longer become stronger than life itself. You now know that if they do, the consequences are fatal. Don't squander the limited time you are given by hindering yourself with insignificant routines that stunt your mental and spiritual growth. Ignite the fire within your soul that will allow you to live the unique tailor-made life that your Creator intended you to have.

FALSE SENSE OF VICTORY

In Wikipedia, a Pyrrhic victory is defined as a victory that inflicts such a devastating toll on the victor that it is tantamount to defeat. Someone who wins a Pyrrhic victory has been victorious in some way. However, the heavy toll negates any sense of achievement or profit.

Living in our society, it is so easy to become complacent and have a false sense of security because you believe that you are successful and comfortable. Then when the major attacks of life occur, you are devastated mentally. There's no counterattack strategy in place. No matter how much talent or experience you possess, if you can't gain control of your mind, you'll never achieve great things. You can't reach the next level of success unless you believe you're capable of accomplishing much more. If you are not equipped with mental fortitude at all times, the enemy within will seek and destroy you even if it appears as if you are on top of the world.

Nothing has a greater impact in your life than what you believe. Your results in life are a reflection of your beliefs. Believing that your challenging circumstances are stronger than your will to overcome them will cause you to lose every single time. Not because life's challenges are stronger than you are. You'll lose because you don't believe that you can win, that you deserve to win.

It is never easy when you face difficulties or challenges. I have to admit that my job situation was extremely disheartening for a while. I was struggling with feelings of discouragement and defeat. Although I am typically a very positive person, the career challenges had brought me to a crisis of disbelief in myself, but also to a turning point. As I made preparations to vindicate myself against the malicious adverse actions targeted at me, it made me realize that I have a higher purpose that went far beyond any position within a corporation.

Liberation Is Imperative

While focusing on achieving success, you must be aware that ultimately possessions, people and situations are not the determining factor. This can be a delusional fiction derived from an egotistical viewpoint, which will lead to ignorance and desolation. The determining factor has to be the internal strength of character to handle successes and victories, failures and setbacks truthfully, with humility and admiration.

When you encounter conflict in life, you tend to want to take it personally and believe that you can right it with your own strength. You want the battle to stop, so you try to control the situation or make a person behave a certain way. The key is to take the offensive within your own mind and take accountability for what you're allowing to deceitfully rob you of your joy. Then taking the defensive and guard your mind daily with reaffirming empowering beliefs.

You are what you believe. Your results are a reflection of what you believe. If your beliefs do not promote you to your higher calling in life, then you are in imminent danger of living a disempowering life, no matter what opportunities come your way. If you desire the victory over the problems and the obstacles you face in the quest of your purpose and destiny, you must believe you are greater than any conflict and adversary that you may face in this life. Total victory can only be achieved through this mentality.

Believe that you are absolutely designed for success and every obstacle is actually a guide towards success to help you learn and grow further. Have confidence in yourself and believe that in every situation, the best intensions of everyone involved is for you to reach your greatest success.

Life does not happen to you, but is a result of how you respond to opportunities and challenges.

IMMUNE TO INNOVATION

You see it all the time in your life. Change is constant and if you aren't willing to adapt well enough and fast enough, you will become stagnant and risk becoming extinct. The resistance to change robs you of the opportunity of personal growth. Change is unavoidable and necessary in discovering new insights about different aspects of your life.

I believe most people do not want to be left behind. They want to succeed, and they want to make a difference in the world. I witness this hunger and desire for it in my audiences all the time, especially when we engage in conversation about better tools for self-discovery and decision-making. The excitement for new changes within their lives and their sense of urgency to enhance their psyche is a powerful scene.

Liberation Is Imperative

The world will constantly try to push you off your path. Your mind will join forces with cynical words and self-limiting beliefs to avoid being uncomfortable, but only if you allow it to. That's why innovation is a long-term commitment. You need to take decisive action to combat the inevitable challenges.

Seize every single moment. Do not take for granted that tomorrow is the next chance for you to reform your life. Get out of your own way and decide to live outside your comfort zone now.

If you are not stepping up to life and walking into your vision like a champion, then you are oblivious to the impact you can have on the world and everyone you care about. How long will you allow your talent to be hidden, only scratching the surface, then cowering away when faced with adversity? Is it a nicety to live a subpar existence? This is an investment in your destiny and you are the main advocate to make it come to fruition.

Essentially, you must see that solutions to your most critical problems are not to be found in settling with a paid to live existence, but rather with immense effort and disciplined improvement towards one's self-worth and entrepreneurial endeavors. Arm yourself with the ability to engage change, take action, and become resilient to the impacts of your surroundings. Despite the uncertainty of life, you must continue to have a growth state of mind. This will give you the confidence of believing in your ability to create change within, as well around you.

When you succeed, no one will ever question the validity of your choices. You will be admired by many for your success, though few will witness the enormous struggle you went through to get there. Do not second-guess yourself and question your abilities; but realize that change is required in order to succeed.

Step outside the expectations of status quo, learn to accept the ambiguity in life and live into your vision instead of the problem. This will open up your mindset to approach change with a "how to" rather than a "why me" attitude, especially as it pertains to your circumstances. You are now focused on creating the innovative solution than on the problem itself. Shifting your subconscious perception will allow you to operate and progress with meaning in everything you do.

Imagine today as the most uncertain, unpredictable friend you have. One that opens the door and welcomes you in, but then vanishes before you even get to know them deeply. You have no clue if they will be here tomorrow. Now since your time is limited with this friend, wouldn't it be your obligation and privilege to give all of yourself at every single moment that you have available? Wouldn't you be grateful for the opportunity to share your vulnerabilities, strengths, weaknesses, talent, dreams and faith with this dear friend? As well as cherish everything they have to offer you? Such is life.

AVOID EXTINCTION

The root cause of mental exhaustion is the failure to draw on the power available from your amalgamation with your vision and Creator.

If there is no risk, then there is no reward. In order to break through the threshold of pain in life, you must have open-mindedness to admit to failure and a creativity to find solutions to overcome it and a passion for risk taking. With these traits, you can use any situation as an opportunity to find a path towards purposeful discovery and success. The journey begins with understanding your own unique capacity and seeing that there are real opportunities for them and areas to pursue them in life. Decide that you will manifest your intended level of greatness. Refuse to accept mediocrity in your life.

Once you see the possibilities, then you can explore and set a new direction for yourself, which includes building options for achieving your dreams. Understand that the formula to success is to know that the past is finite, but the future is limitless.

Ultimately, every person has to control their own path to subconscious independence.

Knowing that everything you need is contained in yourself, you must be willing to accept yourself as you are and remove self-deprecating remarks and thoughts that will shroud your mind. You must update your internal language and mindset to reflect what you really want to get in life, because the words you speak to yourself and others are a self-fulfilling prophecy. Make declarations of gratitude, being thankful for everything you have and everything you are.

Many of the struggles of life come from an attitude of entitlement, but gratitude will change that mentality. By engaging in declarations of gratitude, you embed deeply in your subconscious a sense of appreciation for the world around you. This will lead you to a more purposeful and impactful way of living.

In order to succeed, it will require the ability to continuously manage crisis and change along with the foresight to overcome obstacles in defining moments. You can no longer be comfortable just settling within the confines of the situation, letting circumstances dictate your response.

Liberation Is Imperative

Invest the time to understand yourself, so that you don't live a life denying who you truly are. It isn't worth living a lie and being inauthentic, thus perpetrating being happy in a lifestyle you didn't design but were conditioned to believe was what you were supposed to be.

By all means, it is a blessing to the world for you to be your true authentic self. The most attractive thing you will ever witness in life is when you create and evolve into the person you were meant to be from your very beginning.

Make visualizing part of your daily hobbies. You must value this time with the utmost resolve. Work at it tenaciously. Glorify it instead of squandering the opportunity and being ashamed of the process. Getting to know yourself allows you to delve into the source of joy beyond your imagination.

Being self-aware can help you to plan development and make life decisions that are right for you. Recognize and accept there are things you'll never understand. But continually question yourself. The answers you can think of will teach you more about yourself than anything that you will ever have someone else tell you.

In the next chapter, I will examine more closely the Mental Battle itself. Why is your mentality in a battle in the first place? What influences play a part in this battle that impact your physical life?

CHAPTER 2

MENTAL WARFARE: THE BATTLE WITHIN

> "If there is no enemy within, the enemy outside can do us no harm."
> - African Proverb

SLEEPING WITH THE SERPENT

Your own mind is sabotaging your path to greatness and happiness, but you don't even know it. Silently in the backdrop of your subconscious garden, it is seductively and persistently chiseling away at the foundation of your divine destiny. It's only motivation is to seek out and destroy your dreams. As a master of your own fate, it's up to you to decide whether or not you are seduced and influenced against your will to miss out on the opportunity to have a great and joy-filled life.

To reach your dreams, you must first decide which force you want to be influenced by. Your external and internal influences have a profound effect upon your subconscious mind. It takes careful observation and dedication to learn how best to defend your mentality against the seductive and sly foe of negative influences, which will shed its skin and return even stronger, even as you make maneuvers to release old ways of thinking that don't edify your life.

The secret elusive workings of the mind will make it difficult to detect its chicanery and will instead, have you playing it safe, living a cautious but unfulfilling life. Having you believe that where you are at this moment is the best place for you to be and that anything beyond this life is impossible. It will turn your positive thoughts into negative ones that will prove to be self-limiting. That is why you must be willing to wake up every day and take every thought captive, in order to create the awareness to read, grasp and control them.

There must be a rebirth in your mindset in order to have a new beginning. Through constantly monitoring what you allow into your mind to dwell on will create a purification of your potential. You will begin to override the worry, doubt and fear that has hindered you from changing. With faith, you'll experience a sense of meaning and adventure.

To be truly deceived, one must believe the lie that the mind tells it. Deceiving yourself about your own true passion puts self-imposed blinders on the life you were created to live. Then you go through life with a limited perspective based on your restricted thoughts and beliefs. Not knowing the reality that you could create for yourself, simply because you are assuming that the circumstances you were given is your only option. This will keep you from learning and growing. You will ignore the opportunities all around you and lose focus on your vision. All because you have made the decision to allow your perception of daily challenges to control you.

Ignorance is not bliss, especially when it comes to knowing your enemy, since you don't know what you don't know. The key must be to truthfully evaluate yourself, identifying and acknowledging the extreme subtlety of your mind. The better you know your own patterns of thinking, the more likely you are to recognize and resist the mental assaults that would put you back into a negative frame of mind.

Regardless of whether you are aware of it or not, you are a target because of the greatness within you. Somewhere in the shadows of your subconscious, self-defeating attacks are waiting and planning for the moment when they will strike, catching you off-guard. Arm yourself with the knowledge of understanding and the shield of faith, as these can be powerful sources of protection against this negative thinking and self-talk.

Kevin Knight

PSYCHOLOGICAL HONEY TRAP

Oh how sweet the sound of conformity is to the mind, luring people into a life sucking existence of compromises and selling themselves short. Inserting its stronghold on all ambitions and conquering the call to greatness with delusional ignorance. Without the developed mindset, there is no way to have an incentive to walk away without indulging in counterproductive behaviors. Manipulated by the comfort of being just like everyone else, there is a push and pull internally. Disruptive prejudices develop, which hinder your ability to make good, rational decisions, but contribute to unproductive thinking. Then you tend to fixate more on negative news than positive news. Eventually, you fall victim to talking yourself out of your own dreams.

This is best illustrated by a story I have shared with my audiences about the Miser and his gold.

Once upon a time, there was a Miser who used to hide his gold at the foot of a tree in his garden; but every week he used to go and dig it up to gloat over his riches. A robber, who had noticed this, went and dug up the gold and fled with it. When the Miser next came to gloat over his treasures, he found nothing but the empty hole. He tore his hair, and raised such an outcry that all the neighbors came around him, and he told them how he used to come and visit his gold. "Did you ever take any of it out?" asked one of them. "No," he said, "I only came to look at it." "Then come again and look at the hole," said a neighbor; "it will do you just as much good." Wealth unused might as well not exist.

The areas of your life where you feel most confident are the areas in which you are most likely to develop overconfidence. You assume that what you are doing with your true gifts and talents is enough. But you must consistently develop them, challenge and empower yourself to gift the world with them. If you don't, it is as if they never existed in the first place.

If you sincerely care about making a difference in your lifetime, you must avoid anything that tends to discourage you or to rob you of the pursuit of your passion, which is the origin of your energy and vigor for life. You must be resolute and not governed by what your mental lies and the opinions of others try to push you to believe.

Notice how easy it is for you to have a natural intuition of the riches you possess. Now notice how impossible your mind makes it to truly uncover them and share them with the world. To combat this effectively, you need to understand the truth about what God has ordained you with. When feelings of incompetence arise, you can quickly deflect the deception by asking yourself, "Who am I not to be great?"

Once you can determine that you are a promise-driven person, you will lead a life filled with the ordinary, everyday challenges to this faith. However, you will go places and do things that ordinary people will miss. This is because promise-driven people see and avoid the mental dangers and traps that can erode their faith. Consequently, they are empowered by the same set of circumstances that pull others down.

Always reevaluate and exam your presumption about how you are utilizing your gifts in this world. As time goes on, don't just assume your current actions are enough. In general, if you think you are giving better than average effort at something, the reality is that you may not be, and if you think you are giving below average effort, you may be doing better than you think. Allow yourself to be in a state of mind where you believe in yourself no matter what and continually challenge yourself. Avoid being conditioned to think that your riches are not good enough to excavate and gift the world with. In order to enjoy more, you must think more plentifully. Living plentifully must begin in your mind.

RUTHLESS DECEPTION

The ultimate covert maneuver one can be manipulated into if the mind has been negatively infiltrated and warped is to live without meaning. Deception is more than just an insightful fable, such as I discussed in the previous section. It is a powerful source being given energy through your ideas and thoughts, which influences you into believing that it is real. When regularly fed and affirmed by your actions, it ensures treachery within your spirit.

In Sun Tzu's "The Art of War", he states that all war is based on deception. As you can see now, it is one of the mind's most powerful weapons. It can mislead and make you think that life is miserable because of your current situation, or where you came from, or what failures are in your past. You must learn how to recognize your mind's deception and develop the right mindset to counteract that deception.

Two major steps to begin overcoming deception are:

1. Stop giving into the lies you've been telling yourself and internally blaming others for being unmotivated, not smart enough or being at a disadvantage. In reality, the reason you don't succeed is that you don't provide yourself with enough guidance, support and work to develop the skills

necessary to achieve your goals. So much valuable time is wasted because you let yourself believe that it is someone else's fault, not your own.

2. Forgiveness. This begins with yourself and involves letting go of toxic feelings about your errors, not holding onto past disempowering events, and viewing yourself in a more positive manner. Think kind thoughts toward yourself and show yourself some compassion. Begin speaking to yourself with love and kindness.

An icebreaker exercise I have my audience do frequently is to turn to the person next to them and say, "I love myself soooooo much!" and then I have them turn again to the person next to them and say, "As you should, baby." This always leaves smiles on their faces and the place is filled with laughter. Make it a goal to say this to yourself every morning in the mirror. Your willingness to approach this exercise with the utmost light heartedness will be the key to it being effective for your psyche. You are worthy of your own love and forgiveness. Believe it with every fiber of your being.

Subsequently, the following benefits are typical rewards to practicing this exercise routinely:

- You will build trust in your abilities and awareness of your intuition.

- You will develop discernment about with whom you spend your time with.

- You will become more resilient to obstacles and will cope with them more effectively.

When you are more adept to deciphering deception, you become expectant of your true calling, believe in yourself and are more willing to commit whole-heartedly to your vision and mission in life. Whatever you want to achieve in life, that journey begins with developing your character within. This enables you to deal with the hard-hitting times and supports you to create a fortified mentality toward the lies one can fall victim to.

As Rudyard Kipling states, "Of all the liars in the world, sometimes the worst are our own fears."

ENTICE THE INNER LION

Greatness fears no consequences. The cultivation of your willpower feeds your inner strength. Time and again, I have sat across from people in coaching sessions who have told me something like this, "I will never take that risk again. Never!" Then only to find out later that the person has the ability to overcome their fears and try again. Or someone will tell me, "I will never give my time and money into developing myself, it doesn't make any sense!" and then will discover that they have a gift that when properly honed will be a powerful instrument. Why would someone who is equipped by God with unlimited talents not embark on their dreams? And why would someone with the ability to share this gift with the world become so reluctant to take the risk?

This basically happens because they are not aligned with their God-given strengths. The past trauma has built a pain reservoir deep into their psyche immobilizing them. That discomfort acts like a trigger. Anytime an opportunity is presented to exercise their gifts, the mind counteracts it by activating that past trauma. In order to have a transformation of the mind, one must not conform to the negativity of the inner world. You must become lion-like, extremely territorial and willing to defend to death your mental territory.

Liberation Is Imperative

Give yourself the permission to dig deep and fight the fear within with all of your might and do not hold back. The fear will subside day by day and eventually you have become a different creature.

This will separate you from the pack and the daily monotonous of sameness. Be vigilant because you cannot get through life without collecting an enemy or two with this pursuit. You will make it your goal to positively interact with everybody, but some people will be envious. Jealousy and weakness in others will create bad blood and put you at odds with them. Some people will simply just not like you, and that's okay, no matter what you do they probably never will like you. On the flipside, you might not be too keen about them, either, but somehow you have to face the fact that even though your intention is to partake in peace, you will have enemies.

This will be fatiguing at first, but its purpose is for your inner growth. You must be relentless on how you spend your time. Focus on the activities that grow your self-development and talents. Concentrate on things that increase your well-being and the quality of your life.

Often you will find "clues" helpful in these situations. Depending on the situation, the clue will come in the form of verbal, spiritual or visual guidance. Regardless of the type, it will be powerful and unique. Use this clue when you find yourself thinking about the outcome instead of the journey or the expectations instead of the accomplishments. If you want to control how these situations effect you, the clues will remind you to relax and take charge.

There are many aspects of life that you can't control, so don't let your mental fortitude be one of them. Learning to focus and getting the most out of yourself mentally, especially during the trials and tribulations of life, depends on your ability to allow them to uplift you instead of dismay you. Your mind is a powerful asset to your existence; make sure you give it the opportunity to ascend and support you when you need it most. Remember no one has the right to dictate to you who you will be or what you will become. As you align your being with your God-given strengths; friends, failures, successes and fear will come and go but your enemies will also accumulate. Prepare to gather your inner strength and stand firm on your territory of dreams and be ready to remain steadfast until there is nothing left to war against it.

CAPTURE THE DOUBT

At some point in your life, you decided to listen to your intuition and follow your dreams. But then the critics in your life quickly started to cut you down. Then you internalized these negative messages and repeated them back and self-doubt began to infiltrate your ambitions. Unconsciously, you began to question your knowledge and abilities in everything you attempted.

That self-doubt will never go away. It will taunt you when you set out to make a difference within yourself and in the world. It will devalue your every accomplishment. Then begin to devour your confidence, negate sound reasoning from your mind, and steal happiness from your soul. Then the limitations of insecurity and fear join in.

But by walking through the doubt and into the fear, you will free yourself in spite of them.

Not just wanting the doubt to go away or positive thinking will cut it. You have to go out and take it on with every ounce of ability within you. You must be fully invested into succeeding and deciding that you will not be sidetracked by the distractions. Don't let self-doubt derail you from what you set out to accomplish. You are solely responsible in preventing this. How powerful is that!

When left unchecked, self-doubt will begin to have damaging consequences on your psyche. Embrace the hard work that's a part of this journey and delight in the solace of your resilience. One story about overcoming doubt I share on stage is how I became friends with someone that worked for a law firm. He wanted to branch out by starting his own legal consulting business. He worked daily for the firm as an attorney but wanted to create his own destiny. He was doubtful to go it alone; afraid that he wouldn't be able to make enough money to leave his position and support his family. His main obstacle to be successful was not his talent; it was his belief in himself.

For him, most of his friends and family doubted his ability to be an entrepreneur and recommended that he should just give up on the business venture and keep his job because it was safe, secure and predictable. Despite the lack of support, he did not allow it to poison his mind into a state of hopelessness and give up on his dream. While he continued to have nagging doubts about what he really wanted to do, his desire was totally supported by a new mentor.

His mentor gave him encouragement, made time available whenever he had questions or needed suggestions, or just to talk about entrepreneurial challenges. Though he had all the right plans and capability to succeed, he remained his own worse impediment. The good news is that he was unrelenting even though besieged by self-doubt. He persisted and quit his law firm and gave it go anyway.

Liberation Is Imperative

What he conquered was more than the concerns around emerging out on his passion; he conquered his own trepidation, his own self-doubt. He succeeded because he did not listen to the pessimists; he succeeded because he overcame the greatest obstacle… his own belief in himself.

The mind is really good at coming up with excuses on why whatever you are going after will not work. As you are attempting to live the best life, your voice inside is predicting the worst outcome possible. Just remember no matter how long it takes you or how far the distance, you are doing more than you did before and that's the reward. This will help you find your way back to your vision whenever you get discouraged. In the end, it's about giving yourself a chance.

EMBRACE SURRENDER IN ORDER TO LIVE

If you want to improve yourself, you need to tame your subconscious, not fight with it. There is no victory in resisting. By not submitting, you're walking into a battle you're sure to lose.

As I discussed before, your biggest enemy is your subconscious mind. You need to continually surrender your control of perceived outcomes towards life's timing and the whats, whens, hows and whys. Instead, you need to have unconditional acceptance and total commitment to the vulnerability of life.

Sometimes you avoid surrendering, because doing so would mean relinquishing areas of your life that you think you have control over. You also try to convince yourself that you can manipulate your current situation and control the outcome. But in order to embrace surrender, you have to start with a whole new understanding of what is important in life.

When you accept a situation for what it is, rather than trying to control it according to your expectations, it allows whatever is going to come into your life to do so and manifest its purpose. Surrendering isn't about giving up or submitting or losing, it's not about subservience or avoidance. It's about letting go of what you can't hold onto in the first place; it's about accepting life in the short term and the long term, accepting and receiving each moment for what it can offer.

You must redefine what is valuable and have a quality plan. This will allow you to have a moment by moment choice to prioritize what you really want.

Letting go frees you to be who you really are, to see the true talent within, and the power you were blessed with. This is not a sign of weakness. It is a sign of strength.

Liberation Is Imperative

If there are certain trials in your life which you are having trouble accepting, make it a priority to surrendering your judgement of them daily. It can help you make peace with the difficulties, as you do your best to improve the situation.

Basic guidelines to follow are:

- Accept every challenge even though you don't understand why you're going through them.

- Release the notion that things will happen when you want them to and accept that everything will manifest in its due time.

- Accept every experience, knowing that the outcome is for your eternal advantage of living your true purpose.

- Acknowledge that you must embrace each moment as a blessing, because tomorrow is not promised.

Each day surrender your control on the outcomes of life and do not stress on holding things together within the limitations, prejudices and ignorance of your own will. As you surrender within yourself, you embrace God.

Next I will discuss the pivotal monumental force that will take you through the finish line. So get ready!

CHAPTER 3

RELENTLESS POSITIVE ACTION: NEVER QUIT!

"Never… Never… Never give up."
- Winston Churchill

SACRIFICE LEISURE FOR LABOR

Working hard means more than just giving extra effort; it represents a lifestyle, attitude and desire. It requires sacrifice, a "do whatever it takes" mentality, a willingness to resist the easy way out and drudge through the problems, and a need to get it done at the best of your ability.

Are you tired of starting over? Then, as Prime Minister Churchill once said, never give into anything major or minute, large or trivial; never give in except to the convictions of your heart and good sense. Care about what you do and who you are.

Demonstrate your commitment to your vision and to helping others by pursuing it.

You will be more receptive to having fun at what you do, especially if you feel that the life you live is one that is connected to a meaningful purpose.

I remember when I decided I was going to run a marathon. At the time, I ran no more than 5 miles a week. My workout routine and diet were nowhere near what it needed to be to get me through 26.2 miles.

I made a commitment to myself and my roommate, at the time he was also running, that I would run no matter what. I knew that in order to do that, a lot of things had to change for me to be ready. My diet, the mileage I ran, the discipline to consistently workout and most of all, my mindset.

The first thing I needed to do was visualize myself actually running and completing the marathon to the end without stopping. Then I set a goal of for how fast I wanted to run the race in. I asked my roommate to be my accountability partner. Created a running routine schedule and not wavering from it, as well as pushing through on the days when I wasn't feeling my best or just plain didn't want to run. Despite the discomfort, insecurities and hesitation, I had to remind myself that I had made a commitment to achieve my goal.

Then outside of my personal goals, I found a bigger reason to run for.

A friend invited us to run for a charity organization named FIVE ACRES, whose mission is to promote safety, well-being and permanency for children and their families by building on their strengths and empowering them within their communities. They work to address and heal the trauma that affect children and their families, so that children can grow safely and thrive within a loving family.

Now my approach to the entire event had become extremely meaningful. My own egotistical intentions had been galvanized with a grandiose movement that went far beyond my limited vision at the time.

As daunting as I had made the regimen out to be, I'd now found a new vigor and an internal reward for sacrificing my leisure for the labor of a greater purpose.

All of a sudden it became a fun-filled exciting event with the opportunity to positively impact others that I didn't even know and would never even meet.

LISTEN TO THE SILENCE

One thing I remember, while training for the marathon, was the tranquility I experienced within the early dawn and late night runs. I would take a moment to quiet the chatter within my mind that was causing me to wonder if it was really worth it. I would stand still for a moment and go inside myself, readying to go into the unfamiliar and the unknown. It's an amazing feeling to get intimate with the silence within your soul and listen to your intuition. Some of your best notions will come when you allow yourself to focus in on the melody of the silence. You must tune out the emotions. Do not over intellectualize when you have these moments. It is a restful haven where you come into union with your Creator. You will find sanctuary in the solitude.

"Listening is the beginning of prayer." - Mother Teresa

It doesn't necessarily mean dead silence. It's possible to harness stillness within the madness of life. In the times of your frustration, disappointment, and discouragement, you can find comfort in being alone; not lonely; but alone.

I found myself, in these moments of solitude, being fortified by the purpose of being in the present moment and having a keen awareness of every breath with each stride I made. The doubt

Liberation Is Imperative

and angst dissipated, as I was not thinking of the future, not thinking of the past, but just appreciating the present moment. Silence and solitude are perhaps the most challenging and least practiced disciplines, especially with the day and age we live in now. Our day to day is filled with noise, distractions and chaos.

> "The soul always knows what to do to heal itself. The challenge is to silence the mind." - Caroline Myss

What are the noises in your life that need to be quieted in order for you to hear destiny calling? In stillness, you must tune out every negative inner and outer voice to authentically listen and adhere to it.

Stop trying to suppress it or run away from it by focusing on the discomfort, the pain or the feeling of giving up. Use the moment to center yourself and take that first step, which will motivate you to take another and pursue what you set out to accomplish. Discipline along with a bold and abundant mindset is a necessity. Push through the fictional limitations of your lies and fears. Are you going to have doubts? Yes. If you're not having doubts, you're not pushing the boundaries far enough.

Be empowered by the promise that God speaks to you in the sound of silence.

There is a powerful quote by Henri Nouwen that I share with my audiences; which says:

> "Silence is the discipline by which the inner fire of God is tended and kept alive."

Let this ignite your passion, your destiny and motivate you to get outside of your comfort zone. You will realize that the only one that is stopping you from taking action is you.

Because within the sacred silence of the early dawn and late night moments of life, the only key influence that will have you believe whether you will or will not pursue them, is your mind. Venturing out to the unknown and taking risks will cultivate the skills necessary to overcome any limiting thought pattern. You will grow within the silence while embracing it. Discover the hidden talents you must develop in order to raise the standards of your life. This is when you will boldly come face to face with any discomfort and experience true self-discovery.

ENDURE THE STRUGGLE

It takes perseverance to go through difficulties and develop character. You have to be persistently positive to encourage a greater strength and endurance for trials that life will bring. This greater strength will be a foundation for your own blessings and usefulness.

> "Permanence, perseverance and persistence in spite of all obstacles, discouragements and impossibilities: It is this, that in all things distinguishes the strong soul from the weak."
> - Thomas Carlyle

After 6 months of training, it was time for race day. Waking up at 3am in the morning, prepping mentally and nourishing myself for the formidable feat, I was ready. Only to find out an hour later via email, the marathon was cancelled due to wild fires and dangerous air conditions. On top of that, the event would be pushed out 3 months to a date to be determined.

Now what? Should I just say it wasn't meant to be? That this was a "sign" that I should stop and that I was taking on too much anyway? Give up on my goals and dream of competing in a marathon, taking a consolation attitude of, "Oh well I did my best, it just didn't work out?" Or should I have an empowered mindset and see this as an opportunity to train further and be better prepared for it?

> "I will prepare and someday my chance will come."
> - Abraham Lincoln

I opted to have the empowered mindset and kept training for the unknown date, which was just temporarily delayed.

Finally, after the unexpected digression, it was actually go time. There I was with over 9 months of training, my mind and body psyched to conquer the terrain. My faith was ready to be tested. And then I said hello to mile 21.

The moment I said to myself, "Wow this is the furthest I have ever run," a dreadful pain shot through my right hamstring and my body started to betray me. This wasn't supposed to happen. I dedicated so much of my time, hard work and effort to training.

But there I was finding myself succumbing to the circumstances. I was giving into my psyche, mentally abusing myself. I was actually cursing at myself saying, "How much of an asinine idea this was!" Now I would have to endure this pain and not even finish.

All the work I put in was forgotten and I was blind to fact that I was so close to the finish line, because I allowed the pain, fear, doubt and discomfort to take over. I dejectedly yelled to my roommate, "I can't make it. I got a cramp. I gotta stop."

Liberation Is Imperative

Then in return I heard him reassuringly yell, "Don't stop! Keep running! Run through it!"

> "Sometimes you've got to believe in someone else's belief in you until your belief kicks in." - Les Brown

I kept repeating to myself, "Don't stop." "Don't stop." "Don't stop." Suddenly what I was telling myself took a hold of my mind, and I believed it, and I knew I wasn't going to stop. Then the pain disappeared, I found my second wind and paced strong through the finish line.

The things that you put in your mind are going to show up in your behavior. It is that simple. Whether it is in the words you speak or your actions. Take time to evaluate every thought and choice that you make.

To the idea that somehow when you become diligent and focused on your goals and dreams, you will be free from obstacles is just not true. That's why you need to know the purpose in your trial.

As I said before: "If you allow yourself to, you will talk yourself out of living your dreams."

Whenever you encounter trials, think ahead to the amazing possibility that is beyond the pain, fear and doubt. Begin to think forward to discovering the purpose in your life.

CHASM BETWEEN FAILURE AND SUCCESS

I believe there is little difference between success and failure, especially if you use both to stand firm and walk again in the fullness of the divine life that has been designed for you. Everyone wants to discern the secret and it simply comes down to your perception of a success or failure, when it occurs in your life.

> "Success is nothing more than a few simple disciplines, practiced every day; while failure is simply a few errors in judgment, repeated every day. It is the accumulative weight of our disciplines and our judgments that leads us to either fortune or failure." - Jim Rohn

These are some of history's greatest achievers' stories and perspectives when it comes to failure and success:

- Sidney Poitier: After his first audition, Poitier was told by the casting director, "Why don't you stop wasting people's time and go out and become a dishwasher or something?" Poitier vowed to show him that he could make it, going on to win an Oscar and becoming one of the most well-regarded actors of all-time.

> "I do know that I'm responsible not for what happens, but for what I make of it."
> - Sidney Poitier

- Winston Churchill: Churchill struggled in school and failed the sixth grade. After school, he faced many years of political failures, as he was defeated in every election for public office until he finally became the Prime Minister at the ripe old age of 62. Going forward, he was elected twice and won a Nobel-Prize.

> "Success consists of going from failure to failure without loss of enthusiasm."
> - Winston Churchill

- Oprah Winfrey: Oprah faced a hard road to get to her position today. Enduring a rough and often abusive childhood, as well as numerous career setbacks that included being fired from her job as a television reporter because she was "unfit for TV", Oprah went on to become one of the most iconic faces on TV and one of the richest and most successful women in the world.

> "Failure is a great teacher. If you're open to it,
> every mistake has a lesson to offer."
> - Oprah Winfrey

- Abraham Lincoln: In his youth, he went to war as a Captain and returned demoted to a Private. He started numerous failed businesses and was defeated in numerous runs that he made for public office. Today, he is remembered as one of the greatest leaders of our nation.

> "That some achieve great success, is proof to all
> that others can achieve it as well."
> - Abraham Lincoln

- Thomas Edison: In his early years, teachers told Edison he was "too stupid to learn anything." Work was no better, as he was fired from his first two jobs for not being productive enough. Even as an inventor, Edison failed over 10,000 times to invent a commercially viable electric lightbulb, but he didn't give up. Of course, all those unsuccessful attempts finally resulted in the design that worked. Through his failures, Edison is also known as the greatest innovator of all time with 1,093 U.S. patents to his name. His company, GE, is still one of the largest publicly-traded firms in the world.

Liberation Is Imperative

"Just because something doesn't do what you planned it to do, doesn't mean it's useless."
- Thomas Edison

Sometimes the things you pursue in your life don't turn out the way you thought they would. Discouragement and retreat are the most natural and comfortable roads to turn to when faced with failures. You must lean on your faith and believe that these failures are bringing you one step closer to your successes.

CONQUER THE FEAR

Everyone knows what it's like to be afraid. The key is to get into the face of fear, despite the unpredictability of life, putting your trust in God and journey forward.

"For God has not given us a spirit of fear, but of power and of love and of a sound mind." - 2 Timothy 1:7

Mentally, there are hidden fears that motivate us both negatively and positively. They will either stop you from fulfilling your purpose and what you were called to do or propel you into the greatness you were designed for.

Fear of failure causes many people to never pursue their dreams, or try anything risky at all. Instead, they live a life out of mediocrity because it's "safe." Fear of rejection bullies people into being afraid to do anything that could bring criticism or could result in the chance of looking foolish. Fear can be a paralyzer that keeps you from living life to your full potential. You must learn to control your fears or they will limit and even destroy your destiny.

Fear can be crippling if the mind allows it to be. An example is the fear of commitment in the areas of your life that demand ultimate commitment, such as your dreams and goals, in order to obtain them. That's why one must be obsessively committed to action, regardless of any fear, in order to achieve them.

"Thinking will not overcome fear but action will."
- W. Clement Stone

Fear and faith cannot co-exist so you must be diligent in following your purpose, which leads you to step out into areas of the unknown to do something new and lead you to make bigger commitments.

Practice relentless positivity and be the source of your own validation. Choose to suffer or thrive in regards to mental prosperity. Your unique ability to choose faith over fear makes life worth living.

Liberation Is Imperative

Definitive decision-making stifles fear from obscuring your capacity to think clearly and rationally.

> "I have learned over the years that when one's mind is made up; this diminishes fear; knowing what must be done does away with fear." - Rosa Parks

Allowing fear to dominate your decisions will detract from your abundant life, but faith will enlarge who you are and what you can do. Don't run from fear, stand firm in your faith of God and respond to every fear with an overcoming spirit. No matter how ominous it may appear, you will be able to withstand it.

Here's a funny story I tell to my audiences to bring the point across.

One summer night during a severe thunderstorm, a mother was tucking her small son into bed. She was about to turn the light off when he asked in a trembling voice, "Mommy, will you stay with me all night?" Smiling, the mother gave him a warm, reassuring hug and said tenderly, "I can't dear. I have to sleep in Daddy's room." A long silence followed. At last it was broken by a shaky voice saying, "The big sissy!"

Remember sometimes God calms the storm and sometimes He lets the storm rage and calms His child.

FIND A WAY OR MAKE ONE

Prepare to succeed, not to quit. Acquire the knowledge and skills necessary to overcome anything. No matter how vast the impediment or severe the failure you must never give up. Develop the belief and courage within your vision that empowers your soul to refuse to run away during dire times. This is the divine destiny that God has imparted in you, which will pull you towards your calling even when you cannot see where it is taking you.

Failure is guaranteed only if you give up.

> "If it is important to you, you will find a way. If not, you'll find an excuse." - Jim Rohn

There will never be a perfect time or set of circumstances for you to chase your dreams. Relinquish that mindset and act now by beginning to work on yourself consistently. Your dream will come into existence with incessant ambition, along with late night and early morning devotion to your craft.

> "People are rewarded in public for what they practiced for years in private." - Tony Robbins

Liberation Is Imperative

You don't get to choose the course you run in life, as dictated by circumstances and individuals you meet. The race is designed uniquely for you to finish. Your vision and purpose for your life will guide and support you on this course. It will be your natural inclination to choose the easiest route, the one with the smallest hills and least obstacles. Hold your ground and do not give up when the mind wavers.

> "Press on. Nothing in the world can take the place of persistence. Talent will not; nothing is more common than unsuccessful people with talent. Genius will not; the world is full of educated derelicts. Persistence and determination alone are omnipotent." - Ray Kroc

Overcoming your own mental boundaries will require perseverance. It is not just a matter of trying harder when you are fearful or tired, but taking the time to nourish your faith and skills over and over again, until it becomes imbedded into the fiber of your soul.

Now let's embark on the most important factor that lays the foundation to your personal greatness.

CHAPTER 4

BLESSED & HIGHLY FAVORED: KNOW YOUR WORTH

> "Make sure you don't start seeing yourself through the eyes of those who don't value you. Know your worth even if they don't." - Thema Davis

ATTITUDE OF APPROVAL

This is your time, this is your moment, believe it, embody it and live it, because no adversary will defeat you. This confidence of self-worth will come from you alone, so it's up to you to cultivate a spirit of acceptance. You cannot let others define you, and you cannot let the past restrict you. In order to take charge of your life with the utmost confidence and determination, it is essential that you have the faith that there are no limits on what you can or will be.

Others will have their opinions and ideas on what you should be and what can be done. They will feel they know you based on their perception of the person they once knew, and so they feel that qualifies them as an expert on your capabilities. Who cares? It doesn't matter, do not listen to them. You need to listen to your heart and let it describe what your destiny will be. You need to walk through any pain or anger that you have within you to manifest your destiny.

There will come times when you feel it's not possible, but keep going if you want to reach the intention within your mind. It will be reinforced within your subconscious, so that you can achieve what you set out to do. This is what walking boldly is about. This is what it means to have an Attitude of Approval.

Your attitude will come forth in the way you walk, in the way you talk, in your presence and your demeanor. When you walk into a room, people will know what you are about because of your attitude. Your attitude will be what defines you or what destroys you. It's up to you!

What you need to do is look yourself in the mirror and address yourself as who you truly are:

You are a King.
You are a Queen.
You are the master of your fate.

Liberation Is Imperative

You must also nourish this belief within yourself. You cannot expect something to grow if you do not bring it around light or water it. Such is the nature of your subconscious and your mind. As part of the watering effort, you must surround yourself with other like-minded people. I will discuss in more detail further on in this chapter.

There's a "life choice" exercise I use when speaking in front of an audience, where the result is a life altering moment based on their ability to make a decision. When played all out, it offers breakthroughs within one's life.

The moment when a decision is placed right in front of you, you can decide to hesitate and think about it for days and days, thus letting the stress wear you down or you can just decide to make the decision right there and then. Hesitation is not for greatness; hesitation is for those who don't truly believe in themselves. Any successful person out there makes a decision right at the moment. If you know what your vision is and are certain of what is needed to support it, done your due diligence, and acquired certain knowledge, all decisions are either a yes or no. You decide how are you going to walk about in this life and how are you going to present yourself to the world.

You decide!

CIRCLE OF INFLUENCE

Look at the people around you, study them carefully and then look at where you're at in your life right now. The ones who you surround yourself are generally a reflection of where you are in your life right now. In order to thrive, you are going to need to align yourself with the utmost, upright, conscientious, strong-minded, and passionate people of faith.

For your dreams to come to fruition, you are going to need to surround yourself with people who have love within their hearts and are stern enough to hold you accountable for who you truly are.

If you look throughout history, anyone who has come even close to achieving great things has surrounded themselves with other great people. Now you have a decision to make. Life is full of decisions. You need to decide that in order to become who you want to be, and in order to achieve what you want to achieve, you need the right people around you. Have you surrounded yourself with the right circle of influence?

There is a great quote I share with my audiences by Ray Bradbury; which says:

Liberation Is Imperative

"Love what you do and do what you love. Don't listen to anyone else who tells you not to do it; you do what you want, what you love. Imagination should be the center of your life."

At this point, you are familiar with the saying, "What you think you create." The world we live in now has all been started by a figment of someone else's thoughts; the car you drive, the house you live in, the tools you use, the clothes you wear, everything is a figment of the imagination. In order to harness the life that you want, those that influence you on a daily basis have to be those that will hold you accountable, those that will inspire you, those that will motivate you. That includes your family, friends and acquaintances. It's anyone who you spend the majority of your time with, those are the ones that you need to carefully examine. If they are not propelling you to what you need to be in this world, make a change!

Yes, sometimes it is difficult, but it's more difficult to live a life of mediocrity, especially knowing that you have the power to change it. I've had people in my life that were not in alignment with my goals. When I was making the turn to realizing my vision and walking into my destiny, I knew I had to go a different route in life, one that did not include them. My heart was telling me that I could not grow with them in my life anymore.

In the depths of your heart; especially when you're undertaking the journey of self-discovery, you will know whether you have surrounded yourself with the right people. When the times come that you're not at your strongest, your circle of influence will push you into what you need to be molded into.

That's one of the key ingredients to success, like-minded guidance. It's this type of guidance that you need throughout life. You can't do it alone, because there will be times when you become weary. That's when those that are around you will need to be there for you.

ANNIHILATE THE INNER CRITIC

You must sacrifice who you think you are, in order to become who you know you are. That begins with eliminating any inner criticism, which will come in conflict with your greatness. You have the ability to control what you think of yourself. Every time you reach a pinnacle place, the inner voices will come to try to stop you. Time and time again, they will stagnate your progress. Take charge, and say, "No thank you, moving on to higher and greater places."

You are a light, a beacon of light to the world. Your inner critics are the darkness coming to snuff it out. In order to counteract it, you MUST SHOUT that you are an overcomer! You must repeatedly, obsessively reinforce that for yourself by just acknowledging the inner critic, but not giving into it. Everyone faces their inner critics. The pivotal point is, will you allow them to bring you down? In order to mold yourself into what you're destined to become, you and only you will have to allow yourself to move past them. It's a conditioning period. You have to condition yourself to that battle, because it's a battle that you face every day. But through faith, through desire, and through seeing your vision, you will overcome them. There is no doubt that it won't happen.

The inner critic can be a source of motivation. It is a place where you can become creative by saying "Next!", until you start having thoughts that are of encouragement, that are of love, that are of bliss. You tell your inner critic to take heed, because you own who you are. All your desires, all your passions are made for you.

"Nothing can dim the light that shines from within."
- Maya Angelou

Another way of overcoming the inner critic is by saying to yourself, "No thank you, I'm better than that." "No thank you, I will do this!" "No thank you, God is on my side."

Sacrifice who you think you are today in order to become who you know you will be tomorrow.

LAUGHTER FOR THE SOUL

There's an old time gospel church song which opening lyrics start with:

I've got the joy, joy, joy, joy
Down in my heart (Where?)
Down in my heart (Where?)
Down in my heart
I've got the joy, joy, joy, joy
Down in my heart
Down in my heart to stay

The focal point of this song is to reinforce the promise and gift you have and the key is to remember that no one can rob this from you. You have the ability to create laughter and joy, which has been instilled into you by the almighty God. That is something that no one can steal, no matter what the circumstances are. There is a joy within you, which if you allow it to resonate will uplift you from any situation, from any circumstance, and it cannot be removed.

Liberation Is Imperative

Just think about all the times where you laughed so hard, you fell to the ground laughing and tears running from down your eyes. Those are the moments that you remember. The moments when it's pure joy, whether it's a hilarious moment; even embarrassing hilarious moments. It's as a kid seeing your parents together in happy moments or it's playing with your pet; falling in love; getting married or having kids. If you just sit down and truly harness what you've been blessed with, it brings joy into your life. There's really no reason for that joy to be ever gone.

But in life you allow it to happen. You allow certain petty things to rob you of your joy, when in reality if you sat down and thought about it, there are so many things that bring pure joy into your life. Even now, if you were just to smile and not allow yourself to frown, your spirit will be uplifted.

Practice walking into a room, meeting somebody for the first time, saying hello and genuinely smiling at them. You don't know how much power there is in a smile. A smile is a touch of joy. That joy filters down within your spiritual being. It's a spiritual power that can move mountains.

"Joy does not simply happen to us. We have to choose joy and keep choosing it every day."
- Henri J.M. Nouwen

AVERT COMPARISON

You should strive to be like those you admire, but you should not compare yourself to them. When problems arise in your life, it's going to be your true authentic self that liberates you from them. You have to pay attention to who you are and find your own voice. That's the only way you can share your gifts in a unique way with the world.

Every time you are comparing yourself to others, you are not being grateful for what you truly have. If you really took the time to sit down and have a session of self-discovery, you'll realize how truly unique you really are. How with all the abundance in the world, it does not matter what anybody else has. It's being grateful for what you have right now, not looking towards the future. Stop wishing you had it, because you already do based on who you are. You don't have to look at what's not there, look what is there and be happy about it. Be grounded and be thankful. Thank God, because he's the one that equipped you with it. Fifteen years ago, five years ago, and even five minutes ago are all blessings to you. Take that on as your attitude and be happy for it.

I know sometimes you see the shiny things "the fool's gold' and you want that. That's why you have to truly know your vision, because your vision is not wishing and hoping. Instead, it's seeing, it's a premonition and all you are doing is taking steps towards it. Relax, your destiny has already been defined. Look at the palm of your hand, that's a representation of how unique you are. Your soul has a unique print within the universe that will never be duplicated. That's how powerfully designed you are. Embrace it, and understand that the next time you're trying to compare yourself to somebody. Even if you had the same experiences and the same opportunities, you still wouldn't have the same results. Likewise, if somebody went through all the experiences you went through, they would have a completely different result. That's what you need to understand!

"The more you like yourself, the less you are like anyone else, which makes you unique." - Walt Disney

DECLARE YOUR DESTINY

When you mention declaration, one feels that one must announce what their intention is, and that you must go around talking about it. But in essence what you need to do is to know it within yourself. You must have faith, which gives you the necessary patience, so you won't have a scattered mindset.

Instead, you will be focused on what you're truly destined to be. Because you are uniquely who you are, designed to be a force from which you can imprint your uniqueness upon the universe.

You must avoid distractions, because those can definitely cloud your way forward. You must not give into stories, beliefs, and traditions, which help mold your personal mythology. Instead, you have to stay focused and step towards your destiny. Having a positive mindset will become part of your self-fulfilling prophecy. That way you'll walk over all your enemies, especially if you have that type of essence about you. It's truly time for you to start writing your own destiny, where you become the hero, where you have a beautiful journey, and you have the power to design that.

Don't dwell on the past and don't believe the hype. Just be so great that you can't be ignored, and even if you are, it doesn't matter because you know who you are. Therefore, the stories that you used to create no longer impact you, because you'll be living in your truth. This way you will be a new being. You will live a balanced life with the awareness that gives you clarity. Remember you are justly worthy of greatness. All you need to do is add experience to it and prepare yourself for when opportunity presents itself to be able to show off. It doesn't take money, it doesn't take a lot of material things, but it does take the spiritual being within yourself. Just remember that no one can take this from you.

You are here for a purpose. There is not a duplicate of you in the whole wide world; there never has been, there never will be

Liberation Is Imperative

because you were brought here to fulfill a certain need. Take the time to dwell on it, absorb it and live it.

>"It's never too late to be what you might have been."
>- George Elliot

Now that I've unwrapped the keys to the awareness of the mind when pursuing a life of freedom, let's discuss the key ingredient that will create the liberation.

CHAPTER 5

EMANCIPATION OF THE SUBCONSCIOUS

"Whatever we plant in our subconscious mind and nourish with repetition and emotion will one day become a reality."
- Earl Nightingale

RECONSTRUCTION OF THE MIND

Do you live in a dream world or do you live in reality? Reality is what's gotten you to this point in your life. Having realistic goals will not bring you into your vision nor will it help you live a fulfilled life. You must fervently pursue your dreams. Your reality is in your control. You're creating the outcomes that are happening in your life. You may not be able to control the circumstances framing the events, but you can form and shape them into what empowers you and liberates you into a true person of stature. One that stands with integrity, actively and massively taking on life; encouraging others, inspiring others and empowering the world. Now is the time to take heed and create your realm of greatness.

"It's your place in the world; it's your life. Go on and do all you can with it, and make it the life you want to live." - Mae Jemison

Let's look at reconstruction. When something has been reconstructed, it takes on a new shape. As over time, it erodes. A casualty to the elements of mother nature and time. Erosion takes place unless you take preventative measures. At every moment, it is key that you are constantly restructuring your mind to achieve greatness. If you sit there and do not challenge yourself, do not self-educate yourself, and do not step out of your comfort zone, you will erode mentally. Your dreams will erode, your outlook on life will erode, your foundation will falter and you'll become nonexistent.

You have the power to live a life beyond your current imagination. But you must move outside the physical perception you've created, through the pain of various experiences and not be restricted by your small-minded beliefs. If you are honest with yourself, there are a lot of things in your life that are halfway finished because of your current mindset. Halfway is one of the most difficult places to be when pursuing a life of greatness. It's always the place where things slow down. You can begin to see what the final outcome will look like and at the same time you also realize how much work is left to accomplish. You're not quite where you need to be and you haven't quite left where you've been. The labor begins to overwhelm you.

The closer you get to what you set out to accomplish, the closer you get to your divine purpose, the greater the resistance will be. Physical and mental fatigue will begin to set in and this is disastrous. It can cause you to doubt God and His calling on your life. This will lead to you giving up on what you were created to do and choose to live a life of mediocrity instead.

In saying this, it is vital to create the realm that you live in. Think of every thought as a vital piece to your journey in life. Life changes so rapidly that you have to be ahead of it by having a strong mind and will to form the mental outcome, which will give you a life to live for.

RADICAL NEW REALITY

If you want your life to be the journey of a lifetime, you have to see every opportunity as a new reality that engages your greatness. When you are blessed with a vision, see this as a promise and cultivate the necessary skillset to prepare and equip yourself to bring this promise to fruition. The greater the promise, the greater the prep time. When you are genuinely embraced in experiencing a new reality, nothing can steal that from you. That's what you don't realize as a powerful being of God. There are so many blessings in this world that you can turn to and observe a blessed new reality at every moment.

Here's an excerpt from a poem by Jane Eggleston, which I encourage my coaching clients to read on a daily basis.

Sometimes life seems hard to bear,
Full of sorrow, trouble and woe
It's then I need to remember
That it's in the valleys I grow.

If I always stayed on the mountain top and never experienced pain,
I would never appreciate God's love
And would be living in vain.

I have so much to learn
And my growth is very slow,
Sometimes I need the mountain tops,
But it's in the valleys I grow.

I do not always understand
Why things happen as they do,
But I am very sure of one thing.
My Lord will see me through.

Liberation Is Imperative

I encourage you to take walks and ponder on these words and look at all the things you can be grateful for. It could be in the morning, it could be in the afternoon, it could be at night, but acknowledge the natural creation, which is all around you. All of it is a blessing. To be able to breathe, to be able to see the sky, to be able to hear the birds chirping, to be able to hear and feel the wind blow is a sense of liberation.

You will go through tormenting times and devastating moments in life, where everything seems stacked against you, and your world is crumbling.

It will take some soul searching for you to realize that these are just events. You should be proud of the fact that you are able to stand with integrity and not waver. Most people will waver because they want to follow the norm. They don't want to upset the powers-that-be or the status quo. Once you realize that you have the Divine power within you, seeing a new reality will cause you to be steadfast in your diligence to protect your dreams and beliefs. You will realize that there is nothing that is impossible once you're grounded by faith.

Ultimately, this is no small thing. Many people's lives have been marooned by trials, by hardship, by difficulty when it comes, because they don't have a proper perspective. They don't have true appreciation or the proper expectations.

REJECT THE FALSE ILLUSION

Alert! Alert! The life you've been living does not exist, it has only been a myth. Reject the false illusion. Most people go through life believing that achieving the greatness of successes is equated to having a certain corporate position, being in charge of the household, looking beautiful or handsome and having the best of the best. That's how many define success. The suburban house with a family and anything that disparages from that lifestyle is not considered success.

When in truth that picture is not the reality of so many people in this world who've gone on to do great things. Some people are born into reality where they don't have parents, or if they do, they are abusive or not in the picture. They go from home to home, but yet they are blessed with the intuition that there's something greater than their life experiences to date. When people come to realize that the material things in life will take care of themselves, there will truly be a conscious shift within this world.

If you look at all the people who truly put an impact on this planet that we live on, monetary concerns are never discussed regarding the impact that they had on our society. It's the social impact. Therefore, they didn't come from one cookie cutter society or lifestyle, what they came from is a vision, a divine vision that they worked tirelessly, and some would say psychotically, towards.

None-the-less, in order to be truly happy, you must reject the false illusion and create your own vision of happiness. I challenge you to step away from the media and the advertisements that have brainwashed you into thinking that success is one certain image. Success, and you've heard this cliché a whole lot through your life, is a journey, but that's exactly what it is. A journey!

Of course, most desire finer things, and if that's what you truly want, then go get it. But just know that it will not guarantee you happiness. You can give somebody a million dollars, but if they found out the closest person to them died that day, they would not be happy. Therefore, it is looking into yourself and knowing that you are obedient and affectionate to the laws that God has provided for you that really defines your path to success.

FOCUS ON THE SOLUTION

Often one of the first things that you do when adversity comes into your life is to focus on the negative things and all the problems within it. When failure and all the adversities are present in your life, they can actually motivate you, not hinder you and not stagnate your success. It's critical in this journey for you to never lose sight of the truth within this purpose. Instead of just going through hard times, instead of just being a casualty or having a nonchalant attitude toward it, you need to turn it into a gift and grow stronger from it! But in order to do that, you have to focus on what is the solution within it. You have to build that type of resolve within yourself.

Often people let their mentality just go into a negative tail spin. That prompts you to focus more on the problems and even add more problems that weren't initially created. Instead of just looking through them, you need to acknowledge such questions as, "How am I going to resolve this?" "How am I going to grow and become more powerful?"

As I discussed before, failure is never the end result. It's just a step that brings you closer to success, especially if you stay focused and take the massive positive action to get you to that next level of greatness. Remember to have that type of mindset and apply it to your life, apply it to your relationships, and apply it to your businesses. When failure occurs or when adversity happens within your life, go into your sanctuary of solitude and focus on a solution. Alleviate all the negativity from your mind, which will help you have the focused tunnel vision to go where you are destined to go. Therefore, you are the master of how you feel and how you define what's happening to you. Within that moment, you can make the decision to empower yourself.

"If the challenge exists, so must the solution." - Rona Mlnarik

You have to remember what you focus on expands, even if you're going through hardship or you're going through adversity. If you focus on that, guess what you're going to get more of? Therefore, focus on the solution, focus on the liberation that you're going to obtain through this, and that's what you create, because you are the master creator.

One of the exercises I do when I'm coaching a client is to have them write down all the possible solutions for the problem that they're facing right then and there. You don't have to know the hows or the details for those solutions. Just create the mindset of, "What is the solution?" You don't have to really figure it out, just write down whatever comes to your mind without over analyzing. Then when you capture those on paper, it triggers something in your mind and then you shift your attention. You shift your focus into overcoming your hardships at hand. The next step is to deciding what is currently the best solution and put it into action.

COMMIT TO AWARENESS

In order to free the mind, you must begin with regulating your emotions, managing your thoughts and behaving in a positive manner with your actions despite any circumstances or events. Developing this type of mental fortitude, it's about finding the courage and strength to live according to your own rules and then being brave enough and bold enough to create your own definition of success. It's going to take extreme willpower, it's going to take hard work and obsessive commitment and you're also going to have to form healthy habits. In doing that, you're going to have to devote your time and your energy to constantly improving yourself. In developing these skills, they will help you through the apparent times of tragedy and be strengthened through those times. Sometimes it may be easier to feel mentally strong when life is simple, but if it was that easy everybody would do it. That's why it's important that you do it on a consistent daily basis.

Here are some exercises that will help you develop this mental fortitude and help you to commit to this type of awareness that you need in order to thrive within life:

1. **Evaluate and identify what you truly believe in.**
   These are the core things in your life that will always be or never be true according to your vision and your mission.

You have to put intentional hard work behind them. They can change throughout your growth, so be open to adjusting them when they're needed.

2. **Be careful on what you waste your mental energy on.**
   So many times you come against petty little things, such as traffic or someone that is not easy to get along with, be it co-workers, friends or family members. Remember in the grand scheme of things, those are not major issues. Your job and energy should be on service, not only for yourself, but for others that are close to you and others within this world. That's where purpose will come into your life and that's where the energy needs to be directed.

3. **Replace negativity with positivity.**
   There is no better solution than that. At a drop of a dime, train yourself that when negative thoughts come in to say to yourself, "No thank you!" Create something positive and your whole life will shift.

4. **Get used to being uncomfortable.**
   Mental fortitude involves understanding why you're going through discomfort and making it into something that you can harness for your greatness.

5. **Gratitude.**
   The core foundation and gateway to everything else that you're going to blessed with.

MANIFEST YOUR DESTINY

It's time to start living the version of life you were created for. So Ask, Believe and Receive.

In order to manifest your destiny, it has to be in line with the destiny God has planned for you. There is a divine agenda for your life, there is a spiritual agenda for your existence, and this is the assignment that your Creator has created for you. When all your actions and beliefs and attitude are aligned with this track, you begin to realize and come into contact with all sorts of blessings. Things just seem to be working. When people ask, "How are you doing or how is it going?", you can say affirmatively and with conviction, "I'm doing great, I'm doing fantastic, I'm blessed!"

Just know that anything your heart genuinely asks for, even before you get on your knees, they are already provided for you. Everything you need has already been provided for you, you just need to ask, then you need to believe and be open to receiving it. Many people are not truly receptive to the blessings that are in their lives currently. So how can you be provided with more, especially if you're not even recognizing what you currently have?

That's why living into your vision is so important, because it's being grateful for what you have right now, living into your vision and being thankful for the things that are already there for you. In this mindset, there is no shortage and there is no lack. When these things are in order, you understand that you're guaranteed a blessed life, as long as you're living towards the plan that God has for you. There is really no need to having a scarcity mindset while completing your assignment, because it's in your divine mandate to have abundance.

The key ingredient in manifesting your destiny is knowing that it's already designed for you, believing in that, taking action as needed and being patient.

> "Wait on the Lord, be of good courage and He shall strengthen thy heart, wait I say on the Lord."
> - Psalms 27:14

Now that I've discussed the elements that are part of 'The Unveiling of the Sub-conscious', let's talk about what I refer to with my audiences as 'The Three Pillars of Liberation'.

CHAPTER 6

FAITH, VISION & PURPOSE

"Trust in the Lord with all your heart, and lean not onto your own understanding. In all your ways acknowledge Him and He shall direct your path." - Proverbs 3:5-6

CONVICTION BEYOND REASON

Until your faith is put to the test, it remains speculative. You must have unshakeable conviction, which is more than just a belief. A conviction must come from your heart and pull you towards a movement within your life. A conviction is something you believe within the essence of your soul. You need to have convictions about who you are and about what you believe.

As you establish lifelong convictions, the Author and Finisher of your faith will see them to fruition. So live life with a sense of expectancy and be ruled by your convictions, not by present standards.

Kevin Knight

"Don't downgrade your dream just to fit your reality. Upgrade your conviction to match your destiny."
- Stuart Scott

The world needs people who are willing to speak up for downtrodden and stand up for values. It needs people who will speak up and are led by their vision. People who will stand up with integrity. The world needs strong-minded people who are willing to stand through the obstacles of life and strengthen their convictions through their actions.

In order to leave one's mark on human history, you must have the proper convictions, and then you must live by those convictions.

When you cultivate the proper convictions, your character will be strengthened. Your character provides you with the will to do the right thing regardless of the opposition. A worthy conviction is not just worth fighting for, but is something that you will put your life on the line for.

Your convictions will go within a deep personal level that will exceed any societal pressure or hypocrisy, because when you get into the realm of your convictions, it will not matter what others think you should do, or think you should be. You will remain faithful to your convictions.

Liberation Is Imperative

When I took a stand and stood up for my rights against what I believed was discrimination, I was told by executive leadership that what I was saying was twisted and untrue. Yet I knew that the way I was being treated was unfair. So I equipped myself with the knowledge and support to move forward and protect myself due to their inaction. In the end, the person who they tried to defend was no longer allowed to remain within the organization because of his behavior.

> "Stand up for what is right even if you stand alone."
> - Suzy Kassem

Convictions have and always will come from your Creator, because it's God who has chosen you to do His work in this personal manner. It can be in a form of personal service, whether it's to teach, be a storyteller, play music, assist the homeless, or visit the elderly. Whether you've been called to preach, to be a speaker, be a coach; or mentor the youth, God knows what's suitable for you. It is your job to listen to your heart and develop within your field of service, which is your personal calling. You will have a conviction that's between just you and your Creator.

> "Now faith is the assurance of things hoped for, the conviction of things not seen." - Hebrews 11:1

LIVING INTO POSSIBILITIES

The difference between living a life of mediocrity and living a life of greatness is the courage to live into your possibilities. It's not being content and complacent on where you're at, but evolving to the next level. It's moving towards what you cannot see beyond in your circumstances and thriving with a sense of purpose.

Challenge yourself to go further. Living into your possibilities is where your power is created. The power to have a vision and a mission and walking towards it not knowing what the outcome will be, but having the assurance within your soul that it's out there. In creating a mindset of the possibilities of what your life can be and who you can become, you start making small changes, which eventually start adding up to large differences.

The first step that is required is to understand and to accept that you don't know what you don't know. This gives you a clearing to commence from instead of starting from an idea of where you think you should be. You now have a clean plate and you can create anything from there.

From this vantage point, you will begin to make slight changes that will impact your thinking. That will change the culture and the people you surround yourself with. It will change the language you use.

It is your responsibility to maintain it and that will require trying different things. Some will be successful, but some will be failures. Be unwavering within the mindset of looking into your possibilities and know that there's a purpose that you're going towards.

> "You do not need to know precisely what is happening, or exactly where it is all going. What you need is to recognize the possibilities and challenges offered by the present moment, and to embrace them with courage, faith and hope."
> - Thomas Merton

In pursuing your possibilities regardless of your circumstances and your history, it may result in that desired outcome. The main point of that is it's going to create an empowerment within you and you're going to excel into a different being. This being has a personal mission, which is therefore going to contribute to you having more of a positive outlook in general.

Instead of looking at the world as a place where you cannot journey off and discover new things, trust your imagination within the confines of your mind for innovation.

Once you cultivate that mindset, everything in your world begins to take on a can-do belief and a I-will attitude. You will start to form liberating thoughts, speak using empowering words, go out and create impossible deeds as you walk towards your destiny.

Because of your belief, you now know that all things are possible.

It all depends on how you see yourself. When you're positively centering your ideas of how you see yourself, then you will start to react on what you currently believe you are. You are then a dominant voice, instead of an inferior echo. You'll become more of a movement than a person. If you focus on what others think of you, you will be discouraged. Instead, you have to focus on what God created you as, because that is the authentic you.

Possibilities go beyond your reality. Dream bigger. Be more.

You're destined to be great. You're alive to make the impossible possible.

UNLIMITED TRANSFORMATION

The adventure of a lifetime begins when the comfortable patterns of your old life are left behind.

Liberation Is Imperative

Transformation is the key to overcoming any obstacle within life that you will face. The ability to change is something that you must harness in order to achieve greatness, because change is something that you need.

It's a simple part of life. When there's a flux in life, that means there is a demand to adjust your strategies. Know there will be times when your plans will essentially need to change and you will need to adapt to the new norm.

You must be willing to let go and not hold on to anything that will hinder your progress and sometimes it will be difficult. You have this within yourself. Change is a real process that guides you to your divine destination. It's a reminder to you to never think that you've arrived, so you do not get comfortable.

One of the things that I've realized in coaching with my clients is they are hindered from changing because of stubbornness. Or because they feel like they are trapped and there's fear due to legitimate past hurt, which makes them feel uncomfortable. It doesn't allow them to harness the true power that they have within them to create change.

What I recommend to them is a three step process.

- The first one being RECONCILIATION. You have to reconcile with the conflict that you have within yourself and within others.

- The second step is RESISTANCE. You have to resist the conformity of the world that you're in and knowing that change is an opportunity for renewal and an opportunity to create new patterns towards a more fulfilling life.

- The third is REPLACEMENT. You have to replace everything that you had previously thought was superficially significant. Replace the anger with love. Replace the wrath with kindness. Replace the jealousy and the ridicule with a heart of compassion, kindness, humility, patience and forgiveness.

These 3 R's will allow you to sing a new song within your heart. After the conclusion of the three step process, my coaching clients realize that the only way to truly change their life is to change the way they think. Through further coaching sessions, I am able to develop a series for them that are based on transformational guidance. They then begin to learn about their habits, their truths and characteristics that enable them to create a lasting change within their life.

Be certain that the path you're following is enabling you to become a transformed person. That the path you are following allows your spirit to be aligned with God. Working on yourself and transforming your life will allow you to become an expression of your perfect, loving, meaningful purpose.

> "Life begins at the end of your comfort zone."
> - Neale Donald Walsch

ESSENCE OF LIFE AND SUCCESS

The primary objective of life is to impact at least one person with the passion of your soul as a message that will vibrate on such a tremendous frequency, it will resonate with other souls and impact the lives of all those around them.

To accomplish this, you need to be your authentic self and align with a like-minded community. Your inner circle will keep you focused and help you abound. You only need one or two people to truly make a difference, especially when starting on a purposeful journey in life. You can then take the message of your soul to the world and create an enormous difference.

Many people go through life questioning, "What is the essence of life?" Asking whether they fit into this giant puzzle and why do they exist? Most of these people wait until they're adults to seek the answer.

The purpose of life is to serve and to live your life unapologetically with the gifts that God has given to you.

If you find yourself having jaded mindset, it's because you are sitting on your past laurels, instead of following your true authentic passion and going after the possibilities that are out there for you.

"The energy of the mind is the essence of life." - Aristotle

You must understand that personal achievements are limitless, but that they can never really give you inner peace. Neither will they fill the void of you not having a genuine purpose. That's why you have to look deep down inside yourself for this fulfillment and have God behind it.

Success is not just about you; it's about impacting somebody else with the goodness of the Creator.

If you fail, it's because you've spent way too much time on yourself and in self-pity, instead of just honing your mind. Realizing that you're being empowered by God, who can accomplish anything. That's when you're going to find your biggest joy; at the moment when you are impacting others.

Catastrophe can hit anybody. Sad to say, anything in this material world can be taken from you. So that's why when tragic unexpected events happen, you must have the mental fortitude to realize that your purpose is still to serve. Therefore, no circumstance can impact that, because they have no power over your purpose.

The only person that can answer the question for your life purpose is you. Don't waste your life chasing elusive rewards or worrying if your life has meaning. It does!

Cultivate a deep seeded belief that the true meaning of success goes far beyond the common definitions of success. Focus on the amount of people that are able to live a better and more blessed life because of what you created.

DEFINING YOUR OWN PATH

One life, that's what you have. You do not know the amount of years, you do not know the amount of days, and you do not know the amount of hours that have been allotted for you within this lifetime.

There is not one set straight path that fits someone or just anyone, because we are all unique. You'll never make the perfect choice or make the perfect decision, so why not go after life with all your heart and all your being?

Don't allow your past view of yourself or anyone's view of you to determine what you should be, because you have the power to develop what you could be at any point. So take this life, learn from your mistakes and don't let them define you. Instead, allow them to help you grow into a curious being that is always looking to change the world and take incremental steps to achieve it because it's possible.

"A successful life is one that is lived through understanding and pursuing one's own path, not chasing after the dreams of others." - Chin-Ning Chu

Surround yourself with people who will want you to succeed; but remember, it's inevitably up to you to create your own life of success.

"Time is the coin of your life. It is the only coin you have, and only you can determine how it will be spent. Be careful lest you let other people spend it for you." - Carl Sandburg

Liberation Is Imperative

Defining your own path is spending time within the unknown and not being afraid of it but taking the first step. You don't have to race to get there. Take it step by step, but why not revolutionize your existence and go all out?

"Take risks now and do something bold. You won't regret it."
- Elon Musk

Your attitude and your choices will determine the quality of your life. The reason you are here is to go down the road less traveled. Most people spend their time living a life that was laid out for them and surrender to the circumstances given to them without question.

It you want it bad enough, you will make no excuses. Instead, transcend your pattern of thought and live life on the edge of your comfort zone.

Cherish your experiences and savor them, because in life there is no finish line, there are only growth opportunities.

You do not need to ask for approval or permission to tap into your purpose-driven destiny. In the midst of your challenges, you will flourish. Changing your mental perspective and reshaping your mindset, you can alter any experience and reveal your unlimited potential and gift of abundance.

So nurture your passion, take life as an adventure, delve into your intuition and choose faith over fear.

POWER OF PASSION

Passion is a driving force that leads you to seek the purpose that God has blessed you with. The key is to fervently seek out what God is blessing you with and to begin doing that with all of your might.

> "There is no passion to be found playing small, in settling for a life that is less than the one you are capable of living."
> - Nelson Mandela

Some of the sources to what I call "Power of Passion Killers" that I share with audiences are:

1) Not being truthful with yourself.
2) Not forgiving yourself.
3) Not having proficient time management.
4) Not having a clear purpose.
5) Not consistently nourishing and cultivating your spirit.

Finding your true passion is what will ignite a room when you walk into it. You have the ability to walk into a room and actually bring life and energy into it. Through that you will ignite passion within others, because within the leadership that you possess, you have the ability to help others cultivate their own.

That's where vision comes in. Once you have that vision, you need to take the time and speak your vision with the passion. That is the driving force within it, because people are attracted to the energy within passion. This will help you grow and become influential. New opportunities will be drawn to you because of your passion. This is a must-have in order to be liberated.

Passion is what takes off the limits on what you can do, what you can learn, what you can hope for, what you believe you can do and it also impacts what you want to do and how well you do it. Remember, passion involves having the imagination to see a better situation than what you have now. It also entails having a belief and a willingness to invest in order to make your dreams become a reality. It's going to take sacrifice, it's going to take time, and a willingness to invest in yourself on a consistent basis to achieve mental liberation.

Passion is a lifestyle that never dies.

"Whatever happens, Wherever you go, Whatever you do, Remember this: No one can take the Fire out of your soul, the Stars from your eyes, the Passion in your heart. Those are yours forever." -S.L.

Now onto the next path on your journey, where I will discuss the 1st major foundation of achieving liberation.

CHAPTER 7

FAMILY REFUGE

"The family is our refuge and our springboard; nourished on it, we can advance to new horizons. In every conceivable manner, the family is a link to our past, bridge to our future."
- Alex Haley

UNCONDITIONAL ACCEPTANCE

The inexorable commitment to never withhold love. That is the foundation you have access to when surrounded by the fellowship of family. Family means more than a relationship or friendship; it's not just simply being there. It's an inherent desire of knowing the true quintessence of a person and living for their success.

"Family isn't always blood. It's the people in your life who want you in theirs. The ones who accept you for who you are. The ones who would do anything to see you smile, and who love you no matter what."
- Unknown

Family is accepting of your ways, attitude and opinions, knowing that they don't have to agree with you about everything or anything. And they will, for your benefit, call you out on your "stuff". Without family, you would not be where you are today. Family provides you with the knowledge, wisdom and tools to take on the world despite your insecurities. Showing you the right path, being a motivator and challenging you to live a life worth living.

Unconditional acceptance gives you empowering strength to truly be yourself. It helps you seek out what you don't know and gives you the courage to be molded into the person you are destined to be.

It's time to start crafting a new meaning of family and reconfiguring the roles people play in your world, especially if they do not align with these principles. They must understand that you are unique and embrace who you truly are. That the qualities within you are not weaknesses or flaws, but sources of strength and power. Nor should they confine you to a stereotype of what your success means to them, but inspire you to cultivate it as you define.

> "You don't need someone to complete you, you only need someone to accept you completely."
> - Unknown

Liberation Is Imperative

Now that you understand that a supportive and profound acceptance is necessary to pursue your journey towards success, you must also comprehend that it is ultimately up to you to go forward into your destiny and that is an inward undertaking. I relate this through a story with my audiences.

There was a blind girl. She had a loving boyfriend, who was always there for her. The girl hated herself and everyone around her, just because she was blind. Her boyfriend asked her to marry him. But she said: "If I could only see the world, I would marry you."

One day, someone had donated a pair of eyes to this girl and after an operation she could see everything. But when her loving boyfriend came to her and asked if she would marry him now, she just looked at him with disdain, as she could see now that he was blind too. Thus she refused to marry him. He walked away full of sadness and later wrote a short letter of few words to her: "Just take care of my eyes, darling."

In the end, acceptance begins with yourself, family just sets the foundation.

EMPOWERED EMBRACE

During the hard times, you need to cling on to sustenance that will not disappoint. Creating the space of permission to trust yourself enough to open up to the compassionate words of your loved ones that echo through the hopelessness that you're going through. Encouragement that allows you to see that your situation can change. That there is a better future. That your dreams are possible!

It's the easiest thing to be distracted. Embracing the focus that it requires to obtain your heart's desire is embodied within the others that you choose to have in your life. Just as you would not open your door for just anyone, inviting them into your home, you should not allow certain people or environments into your life. Some people are toxic and some environments are toxic.

They will pollute your mind and spirit, as they themselves are in mental bondage.

Life is about taking a beating while celebrating at the same time. Having a determined mindset and having people who will faithfully embrace you throughout these times is what will allow you to persevere.

Liberation Is Imperative

To successfully be empowered, you will need to shift towards the following five mental dimensions:

- **From solitude to community.** To succeed you will have to converge with like-minded people and not think of your journey as a lone mission, but embrace others in your decisions.

- **From limitation to innovation.** You must create an innovative mindset within your relationships. Getting input from others and implementing their ideas will also help you creatively pursue your dreams and ensure that you transform your difficulties into opportunities.

- **From inadequate to value.** What is important is that you start with what you have now and develop your talents and services, so that you begin to create value for others.

- **From outcomes to appreciation.** Your primary focus should not be solely on outcomes. Shift your priorities to appreciating the presence of good within every situation.

- **From rules to guidance.** Too often you enforce severe rules and convoluted expectations on yourself. In order to evolve your mindset and empower yourself, apply "guidelines" to steer you within the direction you want to go and be willing to adapt.

Your empowerment in life directly depends upon how much of yourself you openly give to others. Embracing empowerment will not only bring a change in your mindset, but a change in your attitude, behavior, and your overall capabilities within life.

SOURCE OF STABILITY

Nothing can replace the appreciation of our loved ones, including having the love, respect and trust from those closest to us. The cornerstone to this stability is communication with our loved ones as a top priority.

Understand that you will obtain strength as you take heed and listen to them. This is the blessing of these relationships in your life.

Having a sense of belonging and connectedness is at the heart of every individual soul. As it creates:

1. Security within your vision and mission.
2. Support to develop your abilities and take risks.
3. Strength to validate your identity.

Liberation Is Imperative

A consistent permanence is vital in your life journey. So remember every day that you have this and develop a habit to do more than what you set out to do. Step into your fears and difficulties, thus growing stronger from them.

This kinship will allow you to have a different perspective from what you accepted before. You will develop the resiliency to overcome the odds in life and be in control of your destiny.

COMFORT IN THE STORM

Amidst the roaring challenges of life, there is comfort the Creator provides that surpasses your own strength. When difficulties attack, have the faith to know that you have what you need to overcome them.

It's a wonderful liberation to know you have family and friends praying for you when you go through the hard times.

It's also important to understand the role you play within them.

Here are a few of the takeaways I give to my coaching clients to counter life's difficulties.

- Assume responsibility for your share within the problem.

- Confront the truth within the problem.

- View the problem from the perspective of your divine destiny.

This approach has helped many of my coaching clients to discover their convictions and strengthen their relationships.

PROSPEROUS HARMONY

Let's begin with a crowd favorite.

Once upon a time, there was a flock of doves that flew in search of food led by their king. One day, they had flown a long distance and were very tired. The dove king encouraged them to fly a little further.

The smallest dove picked up speed and found some rice scattered beneath a banyan tree. So all the doves landed and began to eat.

Liberation Is Imperative

Suddenly a net fell over them and they were all trapped. They saw a hunter approaching carrying a huge club. The doves desperately fluttered their wings trying to get out, but to no avail. The king had an idea. He advised all the doves to fly up together carrying the net with them. He said that there was strength in unity.

Each dove picked up a portion of the net and together they flew off carrying the net with them. The hunter looked up in astonishment. He tried to follow them, but they were flying high over hills and valleys. They flew to a hill near a city of temples where there lived a mouse who could help them. He was a faithful friend of the dove king.

When the mouse heard the loud noise of their approach, he went into hiding. The dove king gently called out to him and then the mouse was happy to see him. The dove king explained that they had been caught in a trap and needed the mouse's help to gnaw at the net with his teeth and set them free.

The mouse agreed saying that he would set the king free first. The king insisted that he first free his subjects and the king last. The mouse understood the king's feelings and complied with his wishes. He began to cut the net and one by one all the doves were freed including the dove king.

They all thanked the mouse and flew away together, united in their strength.

Unity is based upon seeing the value of everyone and providing them with support and encouragement, as well as taking the responsibility to accomplish your goal as an individual.

So far you have been looking at harmony and unity in the realm of relationships and duties within the fellowship. There is another aspect which is crucial to this whole mentality, and that is the aspect of belief. Harmony can only flourish when there is unity and harmony in belief.

A oneness in thought and purpose, where your unique hearts and passions will unite without logic or reason for a common mission, aligned by a divine dream.

> "You don't get harmony when everybody sings the same note." - Doug Floyd

You must allow the melody of unity to flow from your thinking, across your vision, through your emotions, into your actions and personify it in your daily living.

Having harmony does not mean eliminating all of life's obstacles either. With every new venture will come a new conflict of some degree, which is where the growth begins.

However, harmony will soundly provide you with the ability to deal with them appropriately and prosper through the inevitable conflicts of life.

STRENGTH THROUGH LOYALTY

The literal meaning of the Latin phrase "Fortius Quo Fidelius" is "the more faithful, the stronger."

The collective translation of this into English vernacular is "Strength Through Loyalty."

Incredible power, authority and promise stands behind complete loyalty.

According to National Geographic, within the animal kingdom, lions are the only big cats to live in groups, called prides. Prides are close family groups. They work together to defend territory and hunt. The pride only allows certain people into the pride lands and doesn't let vital things out. They protect the inside of the pride lands from outside pillagers. By allowing only useful resources to enter and keeping everything inside away from the harsh environment, the lions work together to protect their home.

> "The most sacred place in the world is your mind. Guard it ferociously." - Rick Beneteau

This type of allegiance within your own life will allow you to conquer any destructive adversary that will attempt to rob you of your divine right to live a life of greatness.

You must create a core group of sustenance and be willing to change it from time to time. Your devoted surroundings should be there after the excitement dissipates and when extreme work and commitment is required.

There will be many occasions when you will need this strength throughout the quest towards your vision.

- You will need strength from your family to nurture you in times of despair.

- You will need strength from your family to encourage you in times of doubt.

- You will need strength from your family to obtain humility.

- You will need strength from your family to demonstrate love unconditionally.

- You will need strength from your family to share your faith and dreams.

The strength you receive from loyalty of family will be your spiritual, mental, emotional and physical anchor. Absence of it will suppress your growth towards your freedom.

Enduring loyalty requires constant evaluation of yourself along with honest and inquisitive analysis of your environment, as it must be aligned with your vision, your purpose, your values and with what your biggest priorities are right now.

It will take intrinsic devoutness to override all other mental preconditioning and consistent commitment to creating effective change within your actions. This will require considerable personal sacrifice.

Based in pureness, loyalty will grant you the exclusive privilege to rule over your mental territory.

As I have now unveiled the 1st foundation of liberation, it's important to discuss the six key elements in utilizing the time you have to pursue a life of destiny.

CHAPTER 8

ABSOLUTE URGENCY

"I have been impressed with the urgency of doing. Knowing is not enough; we must apply. Being willing is not enough; we must do." - Leonardo da Vinci

POWER OF INTENTION

"The Pull towards Success"

Without having a force or an intent in your life, you are wasting your time. Intention is the barometer that allows you to measure your success and draws you to your dreams. It's the grounding strength that centers you and detaches you from the outcome.

- Intention allows you to want more for others than you would want for yourself.

- Intention allows you to focus and offer up prayers of gratitude.

- Intention allows you to see things as an end result and believe that what you need already exists within yourself and gives you a sense of awareness.

- Intention allows you to see life from a gain perspective, and at the same time allowing you to appreciate the abundance in your life, no matter where you are or how you feel.

You will never be able to resolve a problem by condemning it. So you must have the type of focus that keeps you in relationship with your purpose. This will allow you to have the utmost confidence and humility. Having intention in your life allows you to rebuke fear, laugh at the doubt and have kindness within heart towards yourself and to others.

You cannot be focused solely on the results and worrying about what the end will be. Permit yourself to be where you are at and be satisfied with that. In this way, you'll discover what you really want and your actions will support that. Your heart's desire will grow and your imagination will allow you to expand from where you're currently at.

"It's amazing how much you can learn if your intentions are truly earnest." - Chuck Berry

Intentions are the magnets to your dreams. Declare them daily. Believe in them with all your heart. Condition your mind to postulate them and take powerful action to make them a reality. In the end, you must believe that all things will work themselves out, not always the way you planned them to be, but how your Creator *intended* them to be for you.

VALUE OF DESIRE

"The Focus on Success"

Desire is what will keep you from engaging in fruitless activities and wasting valuable hours, minutes, seconds, which you could be using to set your goals and to accomplish what you need to do to escape mediocrity. It's having the mind and heart to make the extra effort, and it's what causes you to face your fears and endure the race.

- Desire gives you the flame to your passion for success.

- Desire gives you realistic and attainable goals and objectives.

- Desire gives you the rationale not to be frustrated during failure.

- Desire gives you the mindset to fight forward day in and day out.

There is nothing more important than your desire to dream and push yourself to surpass your doubt and go further.

It goes deeper than the superficial, because now you have a mindset to have larger goals through your desire. While most people are always wishing and hoping for motivation, you know that type of fulfillment will not bring you true happiness, because you'll be constantly chasing after the next emotional fix. Instead, learn to love what you do and the struggle that comes with it. That type of mindset will lead you to be truly happy, because you will have the WHY to improve yourself and become the person that is required in order to triumph.

Life is hard and if you don't challenge yourself to mental excellence, it will become boring and frequently you will find yourself exhausted with trivial trials.

Raise your standards and create your WHY to give you an intense desire to achieve your dreams.

When times get tough, you will have developed a mindset to go a little further and escape the survival mode and propel yourself into a prosperous mode.

PROGRESSIVE IMPROVEMENT

"The Momentum within Success"

In order to move forward towards your destiny, you're going to need a long term strategy where you're constantly improving yourself and cultivating the right mindset to give you the following benefits within your life:

- Discovery of value and satisfaction within your accomplishments.

- Commitment to your goals.

- Acceptance that your attitude is a choice.

- Obliteration of unnecessary stress.

In today's world, if you're only looking at the short term accolades in your life, then you are only trying to survive not flourish.

So how do you balance your current reality with a need to pursue the constant improvement within your life that leads to a better future?

One way is to develop continuous strategies where you are working on your skill sets and your capabilities as a person that serve others. Then you can effectively engage the problems within this world and stand as a solution to them. You must understand, as you are developing yourself and enhancing your skill set, you are allowing yourself to make other people's lives better as an inspiration.

The basis to you achieving success is a strong and clear vision with a logical applicable strategy that is embedded within yourself. This shapes every moment within all surroundings, because you are able to adopt to a new empowering psyche and adapt positively. This is not just going through the motions, but it is having an honest drive to continually making small incremental changes to make yourself better.

Here are a few steps I share with my coaching clients that will produce continuous improvement within your life.

1. You have to determine your current status within life.
2. You have to establish the need to improve.
3. You have to define and commit to the objectives for improving.
4. You have to organize the resources necessary to support them.

5. You have to conduct a daily analysis on what you've discovered for accountability.

In the end it allows you to identify and overcome any resistance to developing a successful mindset.

THE STRAIGHT AND NARROW

"The Guide through Success"

From a young age, you were always told to stay on a certain path and to avoid malevolent people and disruptive or dangerous things. This sets a guideline for you that should be applied throughout your life, especially when you're talking about the mental aspects of achieving your dreams.

Because any destructive detour will derail you from your dream, it will set you back. You need to understand the cumulative power of losing one day. Days become weeks. Weeks become months. Months become years. The residual consequences are catastrophic, that's why immense focus is needed to stay on the straight and narrow.

> "A person who dares to waste one hour of time has not discovered the value of life." - Charles Darwin

I tell my audiences to always beware of the four 'Ds'.

DESTRUCTIVE DETOURS DERAIL DREAMS.

It may seem like you'll catch up to it. That it won't be that bad. Then all of a sudden, you've veered off the path you set out to accomplish and stress enters the picture. Now you're in catch-up mode and then your focus is not on the moment. Instead, you're thinking about what the past could have been and worrying about what the future will be. All the result of failing to push yourself on a daily basis.

> "Trouble awaits you at every turn when you veer from the straight and narrow." - Linda Poindexter

In the end, it is imperative to have laser focus and constantly develop productive habits that will create your actions. When there's a slight detour and there will be, it's a part of life. You'll now have the strength of character to make corrective measures, grow through it and place yourself back on track.

That's why you must wake up daily knowing what you will set out to accomplish and become. You are fortunate to have one life. You have to take the moments that you have now and see where you can sharpen your focus, so that you are continually chasing your dreams.

In life, there is not one set clear path within the mental aspects to obtain your goal. There will always be detours, just don't allow them to derail your dreams. There will be stumbles, there'll be wrong turns, there'll be bumps along the way, so you have to pay close attention to the signals life will give you. They will allow you to say, "Wait, slowdown, let's start over, keep your head up, stay grounded." You take on this type of mindset and you will make it!

VALUE OF LIFE

"The Reality of Success"

How do you measure something that is so magnificent and precious?

A priceless gift from your Creator.

There is no amount that can equate to the value of life, but there is a price you will pay if you do not truly value what you have today. It's what you do with the time that you have here that's going to be the measure to the value of your life. No matter where you are in your life, you have the power within you to create lasting positive change in every person's life that you come in contact with.

When you look back at the time you spent on this earth, you will see all your experiences as valuable lessons; from the most painful to the most joyous ones.

So take the life you have and go all out towards your dreams.

"The ultimate value of life depends upon awareness and the power of contemplation rather than upon mere survival."
- Aristotle

The true value in life are the stories you create with your life to benevolently impact the world. That's where true satisfaction will come and that's where you will find your passion.

Remember value isn't just the accumulation of material things, because material things will definitely dwindle. It's not just the pursuit of a prize, because that will also fade.

You must be remarkable and capture the inspiration within your soul. Then bring that value to every human life you possibly can.

There is a greater power that has been given to provide you understanding through the confusion, that will heal you through the brokenness, and has made something beautiful out of your life.

Use yours to empower others and create a story that serves humanity.

HUMBLE APPRECIATION

"The Abundance of Success"

The daily practice of being thankful for everything in life is the purest form of humility one could have. I want to impress upon you that the ability to just breathe is a blessing. So wake up every morning being thankful for that.

If you're fortunate enough to see, travel, spend time in nature… that's a blessing.

The ability to hear melodies…that's a blessing.

The warm embrace of your loved ones…that's a blessing.

The support of the people in your life that will never let you quit on your passions…that's a blessing.

This type of mindset will prevent pride from coming in. Pride precedes a downfall and that's what you want to avoid. In order to succeed, you cannot have pride in your heart, but you must be full of gratitude and appreciation.

When I have coaching clients that are bitter and angry either about their work or their family or where they're at in their lives, I have them run through a laundry list of everything they can say thank you for.

In the end, it proves to be a humbling experience, because it makes them realize the countless things they are blessed with and they become truly appreciative of the abundance in their life.

> "A grateful heart is a beginning of greatness. It is an expression of humility. It is a foundation for the development of such virtues as prayer, faith, courage, contentment, happiness, love, and well-being."
> - James E. Faust

Humility and appreciation are emotional states of mind that both help to create the right conditions for a success that is enduring, while preventing you from becoming prideful.

When you are humble, you not only feel appreciation, but also have a strong desire to reinforce what you are living for.

Make time for daily moments of reflection, it will allow you to acknowledge the priorities in your life.

Liberation Is Imperative

Now to have true freedom, the second major foundation to liberation is imperative. Let's discuss this next.

CHAPTER 9

STAND ON INTEGRITY

"The truth is like a lion; you don't have to defend it. Let it loose; it will defend itself."
- Augustine of Hippo

AUTHENTIC CHARACTER

Character is doing the right thing, even when it costs more than you want to pay. It requires sharing your authentic inner self, irrespective of the consequences.

In honoring your own values, you keep your power when you come from a place of truth, despite any corruptive forces you may face. By keeping your word and your commitments to yourself and others, you align yourself with a higher power that will lead you through the darkness and into your greatness.

"Whoever walks in integrity walks securely, but whoever takes crooked paths will be found out."
- Proverbs 10:9

When I made the decision to confront the retaliation of being demoted, I knew there would be consequences. As I was told previously by human resources, that the person who I filed a complaint against was allied with one of the top neurosurgeons in the world. That the "powers-that-be" wanted it to go away. I was also told by a director that the current CIO's only interest was the branding of his department for the health system.

Now the same individuals who were part of the director level committee to promote me just a couple years' prior and gave me rave reviews for my skills and abilities internally and to outside consulting firms that were actively recruiting me. The ones that said they would work to assure that I would be back on the correct career path.

Were now part of the executive level committee conspiring with human resources to justify me being stripped of supervisory responsibilities. I was transferred into a lower tiered position on a team where I had no previous exposure to and that was not aligned with my years of experience and multiple certifications from my previous role. Excluded from further management training and meetings. I was also told by the CIO that I could reapply and compete for a management position, that I once held, when one became available.

Still, I knew that settling for these adverse actions or quitting was not an option. Hence, I stood up for what I believed was right and was backed by not only documentation and the testimony of others but my convictions. So I made it my intent to stand on the power of my integrity, prepared for a long battle and had the faith that God will lead me to justice.

I embraced the mantra of, "There is no one else responsible for my success except me! I create my own reality."

If your name is attached to something, it must mean more than anything in the world to you. From the minute daily routines to the larger visionary goals, you must have a dedicated personal level of commitment. Immersing yourself with this type of discipline will give you the self-esteem to be true to yourself, take in the opinions of others, and not betray your authenticity at the same time.

The key is to expand your mental understanding of what is possible for you and back it with consistent passionate behavior to create authentic character. Then when you are faced with challenges, you will have the instinct and knowledge to overcome the fear and stand on the truth.

"Your ability to stand up for your truth is a muscle, and the more you exercise it the stronger it gets."
- Dan Pallotta

HONEST HUMILITY

The posture of your gratitude is a great indicator of the quality of your humility. In order to harvest, it will not require more effort but honesty. It's similar to planting a seed and allowing it to grow.

If the seed within your psyche is based out of your ego and not from a divine appreciation for the journey you were blessed with, then you will be superficially grateful because your settling for a mediocre mindset. This will take you further away from your true purpose.

Two key elements that I share with my coaching clients to help them to have a stronger with relationship to their self-effacement are:

- Allow yourself the luxury of not being perfect. Instead of hiding and denying your weaknesses, you need to learn to recognize them.

Liberation Is Imperative

- Have an honest reverence to your journey. Respect the fact that your purpose is an intentional design from God and be thankful for it daily.

Remember the journey is to fulfill His plans for you, and not your own; to pursue it in truth not to enhance your own reputation; to advocate for a greater cause, which is not to redound to your own advantage but His.

As a takeaway from my coaching session, I share this poem by Ryn with my coaching clients.

Keep it honest, maintain it humble.
Let it show... From deep within...

Fabricate if you must, adorn with tassels.
First know the seed before you begin.

Let it sprout wings, in your cradle.
Let it soar from emotions and thoughts akin.

Let honesty shine forth from the rubble,
Let humility speak in volumes of what we mean.

LEAD THROUGH ACTIONS

In order to lead with integrity towards your dreams, your words and actions need to be thoroughly consistent. This allows you to have a noble mindset within yourself and your passion. It also builds credibility for the mission you are creating. A great mentor of mine once said, "The way you do anything; is the way you do everything." To earn the trust of others and become someone who positively and powerfully impacts the world, you must first have the utmost confidence in yourself that you will do what you promised in order to become trustworthy to others. Look within yourself on a daily basis and ask yourself the following questions that I use to conduct as an exercise for my audiences.

- What actions are you taking when mental and/or physical fatigue occurs?

- What actions are you taking when no one is around?

- How do you treat others that appear to be unbeneficial to you?

- How do you identify wrongdoings and take corrective?

- Who are the people you model after as mentors?

- Who are the people you surround yourself with for accountability?

- Are you a slave to destructive impulses, circumstances and/or people?

- Are you writing out and reviewing all your commitments on a daily basis?

- Do you do what you should do before you do what you want to do?

- Do you commit yourself to adding value to others and helping them succeed?

This is a process that does not happen overnight. It will take a decisive and deliberate plan that you must adhere to day by day to develop the qualities needed. Then the endurance to constantly adapt and adjust your behavior and habits to them.

The courage and faith you will develop within yourself through this will gleam through the fiber of your being and will show forth to those that you interact with.

There should be an indestructible covenant between your words and your actions. This begins with setting the intention of having a mindset that is grounded and led by integrity. Abiding by your commitments and doing whatever it takes to bring them to fruition.

> "The most powerful leadership tool you have is your own personal example." - John Wooden

DISCIPLINED ACCOUNTABILITY

Self-control and liability begins with the mind.

In order to ingrain the habits conducive to making your dreams a reality, you have to make a conscious choice to abide by the commitments you set out to accomplish in order for your word to become law.

In your life there are a lot of things you don't like to do. No one likes going through the process, but it is in the process where greatness is shaped.

You must take on the personal responsibility to make sure that should the situation arise where discipline is needed, that actions reflect the follow through on your commitments. This includes having the personal initiative to get started and the stamina to persevere despite obstacles.

This requires abandoning immediate satisfaction, in order to gain something better, which will require effort and time to see greater success in all areas of your life.

Forming the habit of accountability will serve as a check and balance system to protect you when your drive wavers and you need to realign to your goals.

Being aware and open to what you are thinking allows you to be accountable for your actions. Doing so enables you to know yourself and your purpose in a deeper manner.

Also, having a mastermind group around of people whom you can trust and know well will enable you to know yourself, your strengths, weaknesses, and opportunities more deeply.

In the end, you must make success your priority. You should strive to make holding yourself accountable to your goals an everyday part of your life, to the point where it becomes routine. Applying yourself to obtain them day after day, and working on them whenever time permits.

FORTIFIED COURAGE

The main obstacles standing between you and your dreams are your fears and self-doubt. When pursuing your dreams, people will attempt to convince you that they are not logical and unattainable. So if the world is bold enough to attack your dreams, then you must be bold enough to fight for them.

"With courage you will dare to take risks, have the strength to be compassionate, and the wisdom to be humble. Courage is the foundation of integrity." - Mark Twain

These obstacles will sharpen the image of your dreams giving you more clarity, and your struggles will make you hungrier. The 5 main keys to having a life of liberation when pursuing your divine destiny are:

- Always declare your dreams to yourself and others. Don't be ashamed or afraid to speak the dreams that God has given you.

- Allow patience to be your virtue as you work towards your dreams. Waiting for your dreams to materialize is a test of your faith.

- Acknowledge and celebrate the victories along the journey towards your dreams. These are blessings that should not be taken for granted.

- Absolute dedication is a must in order to obtain your dreams. You must be willing to sacrifice on every level to endure this quest.

- Appreciate who you are now and know that it is enough to make your dreams come true. God has created every miracle needed for you to succeed. The main one being you.

In having this type of visionary mindset, you will evade a life that is empty and mediocre. Thus, enhancing your quality of life and giving you the courage to fight through your fears and doubts to thrust you into your greatness.

BALANCED PROSPERITY

To have true success you must be able to achieve your goals and balance the important essentials within your life. This is accomplished by challenging your mindset to create opportunities and simultaneously allocating the time to enjoy the true joys of life.

You must elicit the mentality of living a vibrantly healthy and stress-free life. Finding time each day to be alone to quiet your thoughts and visualize your goals.

Focusing on life as a continuous process of perpetual learning mentally, physically and spiritually with a joyful, persistent, hardworking, and disciplined attitude. When your life is in balance, you will find more contentment, and more confidence. You will be unrestricted to be yourself, and not influenced by the expectations of other people. You will have direction, and your life will take on a new vigor. Regardless of what other people are doing, regardless of what is happening in the world, you will remain driven by your purpose.

Living a life of contribution will give you meaning through giving your all to causes that matter to you.

> "You're happiest while you're making the greatest contribution." - Robert F. Kennedy

Your purpose is about what you offer to the world, not what the world has to offer to you. Concern yourself primarily with giving, as well as receiving. In this way, you will find and live your true purpose. Your aim should be to love and serve others in meaningful ways.

When you believe in your abilities and talents, you will end up doing what you love. You will find your passion and the meaning in it. Through working hard at it every day, your mentality will evolve and you will create a purposeful life.

Liberation Is Imperative

Refuse to live an insignificant life and take a leap of faith to living the life of your dreams right now.

As you come to an end on this voyage towards liberation, let's explore the crown jewel to finding true meaning in your life. It's the gift that once you discover it, every day you will feel like you are on a mission.

CHAPTER 10

LEAVE A LEGACY

"What you leave behind is not what is engraved in stone monuments, but what is woven into the lives of others."
- Pericles

BLESSING OF EMPOWERMENT

It is time for you to accept the truth of the foundation God has laid down for your life. You have the power to change the world around you.

Submitting your will to a life of greatness, which impacts the world, will bring you empowerment and the ability to overcome life's adversities. Take the time to discover what it takes to attract the blessings in your life and be the person today that others will remember you for.

"Today I shall behave, as if this is the day I will be remembered." - Dr. Seuss

This will allow you to have the ability and authorization to succeed. The resolve to continue when you cannot see the immediate results. Through the determination of seeking out your dreams with all your heart, it brings the promise of being unstoppable.

You must also come to the realization that in the grand scheme of things, it's not about you. It's about being a beacon of light that emanates from your love, illuminates the passions of others, and reveals the greatness that is possible within their lives.

You must not compromise to the conditioned mind, instead strive to being a person of integrity. Your willingness to not give up and remain determined is a demonstrative example of truth that emits from your life.

Freedom comes from consciously deciding to make a difference within yourself and the world you create.

Mastery of this path will lead to changes within the following aspects of your life:

- You will move into deeper levels of your vision and purpose.

- You will better understand God's power of anointing within your life.

- You will begin to be much more focused about the things that truly matter.

- You will immediately begin to experience incredible joy in your life.

- You will develop a higher level of self-awareness and confidence.

Each day you must choose to have a deep seeded belief in your abilities to keep the possibility of greatness alive. Letting go of the old ways of mediocrity and challenging the norm, you can have the abundance of God's blessings and enjoy the fullness of a life greater than what you have ever imagined.

Stay focused on the promises in your life and not the limitations. Live your life with a sense of expectancy. Allow the Creator to lead you on your path and be the central guiding force.

DEVOTION TO SELF-REFLECTION

Dreams come as whispers and if you are not engaged in dedicated, consistent self-reflection, they will be fleeting opportunities. If the person you are now is unable to take you to where you want to go, then it's time to reinvent yourself.

"Your vision will become clear only when you can look into your own heart. Who looks outside, dreams; who looks inside, awakes." - Carl Jung

Life is about finding yourself and creating the life you were meant to have. It's an infinite journey that allows you to have unlimited creativity in your mind. Your perception of yourself becomes a reflection of how you believe other people see you. In order to develop a mindset of a winner, you must explore the following areas:

- **Define your WHY.** List five top reasons you want to create freedom within your life.

- **Dream BIG.** Challenge yourself to create a dream that scares and motivates you.

- **Develop a YES attitude.** Adopt a positive attitude towards everything you encounter.

Engaging yourself in thought-provoking examination of these areas will help you to understand yourself better.

"Self-reflection is a humbling process. It's essential to find out why you think, say, and do certain things... then better yourself." - Sonya Teclai

Liberation Is Imperative

Reflection allows you to observe your actions and results, based on steps you have taken toward your dreams, as well as opening a space for learning and growing from them.

You are the narrator to your life story. How you want it to be defined is up to you. You set the frame through your beliefs and actions. The insight you gain from this will build solid confidence and create a new and different outlook on your life. Taking the time to self-reflect and look inwards. This gives you the ability to understand your mental strengths, weaknesses, drives, values and goals, as well as recognize their impact on your dreams. Then redirect any disruptive mindset and actions to supportive ones.

You should consistently review your inner thoughts and actions. It takes discipline, but if living a life of your dreams is a must for you, then you need to make sure your mindset matches up. Then no matter what, you will find the time to give yourself quiet time to explore these thoughts and actions, thus preparing yourself for challenging moments.

The main way to start this process is to first stop the racing thoughts within your mind, acknowledge them and then begin to notice all the things around you. That means noticing your surroundings and being present within the moment.

This allows you to see how far along your path to your dreams you've come, and whether it's still best to follow the same path, or change direction and try a new path.

SACRIFICE AS AN INVESTMENT

There are no excuses. You must be willing to abandon the pleasures within your life, to become vacant of selfishness and self-gain, in order to become a shining example of freedom.

This is what will make you stand out. It's a principle that will develop within you a profound love for others. You then become blessed with awareness that you have the opportunity to be a miracle in someone's life through your kindness, talents and time.

Fully committing to being of service will require you to approach your life without expectation of reciprocation. Living in such a way, regardless of circumstances, you can fulfill the purpose of your existence.

Your life will no longer to be controlled by what happens around you, but rather by what's within you.

Liberation Is Imperative

"Learn to love without condition. Talk without bad intention. Give without any reason. And most of all, care for people without any expectation." - Unknown

Greatness requires sacrifices and there is no growth without sacrifice. It's about being the best that you can be.

You don't need to know the exact path to greatness, you only need to be consistently changing and making the necessary adjustments, so that you can walk towards its path.

VALIDATE YOUR VISION

Before success becomes a reality, there must be a belief within your mind that it is possible. Through changing your thoughts that are not aligned to your higher vision, you equip yourself to understand the journey ahead. Many people go through life not understanding the purposes of their trials.

Clarity within your vision provides you with the foresight to interpret the events of your life.

The next step is to break your vision down into goals. These are measurable increments gauging the progress. This also sets a sense of urgency within your vision.

In order to move forward, things cannot remain the same. The mentally you have now will not fulfill your vision. Taking the right actions will be powerful enough to give you the life you want. Because it's not enough to just decide on a goal, you have to decide to reach for it. You have to decide to take what you want. Understand that no one is coming to fulfill your purpose for you.

It will take you owning your responsibility of being the change you want to see.

"You are to make your own way prosperous... Even God cannot do it for you; you will have to do it yourself by doing the right things; making right decisions, talking right, thinking right, being at the right place with the right-kind of people and by reading the right materials." - Jaachynma N.E. Agu

You must be ready to ignite and accelerate your dreams to live the vision you are here to share. A critical part of that is having a clear picture of where you are going. You cannot accomplish what your mind cannot believe.

Taking empowered actions that explore your vision, you will create a life of your own design. Living every moment of your life free and upon your own accord.

BEQUEATH A STEADFAST BELIEF

Believing in yourself takes guarding your mind to become what you need to be to live a life of passion. Ridding it of old self-doubt thoughts and replacing them with reinforcing positive ones.

"As soon as you trust yourself, you will know how to live."
- Johann Wolfgang von Goethe

Here are 6 key steps to believing in yourself that I share with my audiences.

1. Write down all your dreams in detail.

2. Start taking small steps every day to accomplish your dreams.

3. Create an outlined vision map.

4. Write down your daily intentions.

5. Observe the daily beauty in your everyday life.

6. Take action. Pursue your dreams. Question everything.

Success in life comes only if you believe in yourself. If you really want something with all of your heart, it's what you think and believe that matter. You then must take action every day to turn what you see in your mind's thoughts into reality.

FORGE A PATHWAY TO FOLLOW

Life is journey to become the strongest version of yourself. Building a legacy worth leaving behind begins today and is made one decision at a time.

> "I alone cannot change the world, but I can cast a stone across the waters to create many ripples."
> - Mother Teresa

We all will leave a legacy. The impact of your legacy is up to you. Great things come to those who go after them. Make it a lifetime commitment and do everything you can to continue to improve yourself.

You have a choice. To leave behind a life of purpose, you must make your life about something bigger than yourself and pursue it with character, conviction, and passion. In that way, you will find what matters most to you and what is worth living and dying for.

Liberation Is Imperative

Ask yourself this question. If today was your last day, would you be able to look your loved ones in their eyes and say, "Yes, I have given my all and played my role in making this world a better place for them?"

I implore you to not be distracted with insignificant thoughts. You are free once you realize you have been given the power to change everything. You have the opportunity to be and do anything. Elevate your thoughts, change your mindset and you will then change your world.

ABOUT THE AUTHOR

Working in the corporate world for over 18 years for top firms, such as GE, AETNA, DELIOTTE and UCLA HEALTH, holding leadership positions and earning an MBA, Kevin found himself confronted with discrimination and retaliation, later being demoted, left devastated but determined. He eventually realized that he controlled his own destiny and created a different mindset to live a better, happier and more fulfilled life.

Within the journey, Kevin found himself revisiting a past tragic event as a youth where his eldest sister was murdered, a victim of domestic violence. In the process of searching for the purpose within this life altering event, he was blessed with a moment of awareness and clarity. In that he discovered his Vision, which is to eradicate domestic violence globally. His Mission is to empower society to create healing change within the lives of abused women and children.

With his family as priority, he and his wife are blessed with 5 kids, and within 3 pregnancies, two sets of twins!! Kevin now shares his story through speaking, teaching and coaching others on how to discover their vision and create a life of freedom for themselves. Find out more about Kevin at www.liberationisimperative.com.

Kevin Knight

Liberation Is Imperative

www.ingramcontent.com/pod-product-compliance
Lightning Source LLC
Chambersburg PA
CBHW071432160426
43195CB00013B/1873